Morristown

W9-BGA-224

A History and Guide
Morristown National Historical Park
New Jersey

Produced by the
Division of Publications
National Park Service

U.S. Department of the Interior
Washington, D.C. 1983

About This Book

The encampments of the Continental Army at Morristown, New Jersey, sum up much of the Revolutionary War. The American Revolution was a war more of waiting than of battles and fighting. For the patriots, perhaps this was just as well, because they tended to lose the battles. But waiting imposed its own trials on patience and on the ability of the infant United States and its weak economy to sustain an army in the field. In a contest of patience and endurance, Great Britain might have retained her American empire simply by persisting longer in the struggle than the often impatient patriots. Morristown tested the emotional and physical resources on which depended the Continental Army and ultimately the American cause. That is the story this book tells.

All artifacts shown on the following pages are from the collections of Morristown National Historical Park, except for the medical chest on page 61 which is from the Chester County (Pa.) Historical Society.

Library of Congress Cataloging in Publication Data
Weigley, Russell Frank.
Morristown, Morristown National Historical Park, New Jersey.
(National park handbook; 120)
Supt. of Docs. no. I 29.9/5:120)
1. Washington, George, 1732-1799—Headquarters—New Jersey—Morristown. 2. Morristown (N.J.)—History. 3. Morristown National Historical Park (N.J.)—Guidebooks. 4. Morristown (N.J.)—Parks—Guidebooks. 5. Morristown (N.J.)—Buildings—Guidebooks. I. Title. II. Series: Handbook (United States, National Park Service, Division of Publications); 120.
F144.M9W44   1983   917.49'74   83-600148
ISBN 0-912627-21-2

☆GPO:2003–497-153/60512

Officers Present fit for duty														
Field			Commiss.ᵈ				Staff					Non Comm.ᵈ		
Colonel	Lt Colonel	Major	Captains	Cap.ᵗ Lieuts	Lieutenants	Ensigns	Adjutant	Pay Master	Quarter Mas.ʳ	Surgeon Mate	Serj.ᵗ Major	Qᵘ Mᵗ Serj.ᵗ	Drum Major	Fife Major
Total 1	..	..	3	1	4	1	1	1	1	1				
Present	..	..	..											
Absent														

Camp near Morristown Christm...

Dr. Brother — White I believe I forgot
in my last, but however your letter
I was in haste & burnt my letter
... tell, I must ...
... brothers, ...
... over I h...

By George F. Scheer

	D.º Absent	Out Lodn: on duty	On Furlough	Totals		Serjeants	Drum Fifes	Rank & file	Dead	to Inability	Sone Expired	Deserted	Transferd	Promoted	Reduced	Taken Prisoners	Serjeants	D.º & fife
7	6	43	12	7	262		3	"	242	"	1	"	1	"	"	"	"	1

1 Gen.l Green
1 Gen.l Wayne
1 Lord Stirling
1 Col.º Abeals
2 Waggoners
1 Capt.n Dunn
1 Baker
1 Artificer
Surveying
Major Moore
Ant.t Gen.l Hydes

No man could endure [the storm's] violence many minutes without danger of his life. Several marquees were torn asunder and blown down over the officers' heads in the night, and some of the soldiers were actually covered while in their tents and buried like sheep under the snow. . . .

We are greatly favored in having a supply of straw for bedding. Over this we spread our blankets, and with our clothes and large fires at our feet, while four or five are crowded together, preserve ourselves from freezing. But the sufferings of the poor soldiers can scarcely be described. While on duty they are unavoidably exposed to all the inclemency of storms and severe cold. At night they now have a bed of straw on the ground and a single blanket to each man. They are badly clad and some are destitute of shoes.

Dr. James Thacher,
Continental Army surgeon,
January 1780

After marching several days "through cold and snow," barely subsisting on a daily portion of a little "miserable fresh beef, without bread, salt or vegetables," young Pvt. Joseph Martin, 8th Connecticut Regiment, reached the Continental Army's "wintering ground" late on a gray and foreboding afternoon in December 1779. Locally the place was called Jockey Hollow, a bleak, wind-swept hardwood forest in the rough hills the natives call mountains some four miles southwest of Morristown, N.J. For all the marrow-freezing cold and snow knee-deep and his ravenous hunger, Martin was luckier than most, because his brigade still had its blankets and tents. Many of the older units making camp in the silent woods had neither.

Despite the near-zero weather, many of the men, noted one of the army's surgeons, were "actually barefooted and almost naked." For most a little brushwood thrown together and an armfull of buckwheat straw, issued as they filed into camp, were their only defense against the blowing snow. Officers fortunate enough to have horses, however, had at least greatcoats and saddle blankets. As night fell, they spread their blankets on the ground, wrapped themselves in their coats, and lay close together for warmth with a fire at their feet.

Private Martin scooped out a place in the snow to pitch his tent. With only another handful of beef for his supper, he settled down on the frozen ground, protected by canvas from the wind and falling snow, but cold and hungry in his straw bed.

What Joseph Martin, the Continental Army, and its commander in chief George Washington endured at Morristown during the terrible months that followed and how they survived it is

what this book is about. It explains the strategy that led Washington to select this ground for his winter cantonment and relates the frustrations and anguish he suffered in keeping his little army together. It tells not only of the long and dreadful 1779-80 winter, the cruelest of the century, but also of the earlier encampments here, which, with that final one, have made Morristown one of the most significant and inspiring of all American historic sites. Americans tend to think of the winter at Valley Forge as the nadir of Revolutionary Army suffering, but it was Morristown that tested the soul of the American cause.

Lying behind Long Hill and the Watchung Mountains, protected from sudden attack by both those rugged heights and broad swamps, Morristown was a position carefully chosen by Washington. From it, with reasonable security, he could keep an eye on the British wintering in and around Manhattan Island, guard the roads connecting New England with the Revolutionary capital at Philadelphia, and move swiftly to any threatened point.

Anticipating a long cantonment at this advantageous position, he had decreed that his army, upon taking up its ground at Jockey Hollow, should build a "Log-house city" of habitation. Impeded by the weather, the work of felling the great forest of Jockey Hollow and throwing up hundreds of cabins went slowly. Almost all of December, the men slept under tents or with no covering at all; a number were not under roofs until February.

In time, however, some 600 acres of forest gave way to regular streets of huts in broad, open, stumpy fields with but a clump of trees standing here and there. As the soldiers huddled about their cabin hearths, they did find some relief from the unending cold, but there was seldom any relief from the pain of empty bellies. Thus Joseph Martin found himself, after a long snowfall, "literally starved." For four days and nights, he put not "a single morsel of victuals" into his mouth, except, he said, "a little black birch bark which I gnawed off a stick of wood." At dark the fourth day, when rations were issued, he got only a half-pound of fresh beef and a gill of wheat to boil.

Officers, if general or staff, fared reasonably well, but were not without discomfort and the burdens of responsibility. The general established headquarters in the town's most impressive mansion, the great Georgian home of widowed Mrs. Jacob Ford. Here he housed himself and his wife when she came and many of his staff, his official family. General officers lodged in houses throughout the neighborhood. Line officers, ordered to hut with their regiments, were forbidden to start building their own huts until those of the enlisted men were completed. As a result, colonels and officers of lesser rank tented under canvas in Jockey Hollow well into the new year of 1780.

For the commander in chief, whose first concern was to sustain that shivering and slowly starving army in the Hollow, it became a winter of anxiety. Even if supply wagons could have made it through roads where for weeks snow drifted five and six feet deep, the general's war chest was too bare to buy nearly enough clothing, shoes, and provisions for his thousands. The Continental treasury as well was all but empty. And what small funds the general could scrape up didn't go far, because by the winter of 1779 Continental currency had sunk so low in value that many farmers refused to accept it for their hay, grain, and livestock.

Since Congress could not supply the army, in desperation Washington appealed to the governments of the middle States; when they failed to respond, he took the drastic step of levying through magistrates on each county in New Jersey for food and forage, giving farmers promissory certificates for payment. Levying resolved the immediate crisis, but in spite of the general's every effort, food was soon scarce again, compelling him to live constantly with the fear that he might be obliged to disband his forces entirely because he could not feed them.

While agonizing over the poverty of the army and its possible dissolution by starvation, Washington was confronted with the perhaps more critical threat that expiring enlistments would leave him with only a skeleton force when the next campaign opened. The force he had in the main camp and in detachments in Jersey and the New York highlands numbered only half of the force he had commanded the previous winter. And at Morristown, his poorly fed, poorly clothed, unpaid soldiers let it be known that when the scheduled terms of some 5,700 of them expired, beginning the last day of December, many of them did not intend to re-enlist.

The presence of the army at Morristown, considered a "pretty little village" of some 50 or 60 houses, 200 to 300 inhabitants, created problems also for the citizens of the community. The Morristown elite might have anticipated the arrival of the army as an exciting opportunity to socialize with the commander in chief, a hero to most of America. But the majority of the villagers, peering through their frosted windows, could not have welcomed wholeheartedly the sight of the columns of weary and tattered troops

that came tramping through the snow, bound for Jockey Hollow, all during December. The prospect of engulfment by some 10,000 threadbare, shivering, hungry, shelterless men must have been somewhat alarming, for the December 1779 encampment was not the Continental Army's first at Morristown. Three years before, fresh from its triumphant surprise of the British at Trenton and Princeton, the army had wintered in the Morristown neighborhood. Then Washington, in an effort to conceal from the British the actual thinness of his ranks, had billeted three and four men in every house for miles around. As cantoned armies, however disciplined, are wont to do, that earlier army had stripped the neighborhood and laid both hardships and insults on the citizenry. Before that winter was done, the citizens complained to Washington about the offensive public swearing of men and officers, epidemic gambling, and some plundering of farmsteads. That army had also brought smallpox, and to the dismay of the populace—though ultimately it worked out well—Washington had enforced compulsory community inoculation. Thus in this December of 1779 the prospect for harmonious co-existence between the army and village must have seemed fragile at best.

As it turned out, some soldiers did prey on local citizens. In January, when starving soldiers marched out of camp and foraged in the barnyards and gardens of the neighborhood, Washington found himself unable to bring himself to punish them. But when some of them continued, in his words, to "maraud and plunder in the most shameful and injurious manner," he cracked down and ordered that any man found "straggling out of the chain of centinels after retreat beating" shall receive 100

lashes "upon the spot" and any found robbing, 500.

Though for the most part the Morristown winter was gloomy, Washington, who loved to dance, lightened the cares and monotony for himself and ranking officers by organizing a series of "dancing assemblies," paid for by subscription. A social commentator recorded: "Yesterday a Christmas dinner in compliment to the Washingtons at the Chevaliers. Next Thursday he gives a ball to thirty ladies; tomorrow another at Mrs. Holkers. His excellency intends having concerts once a week at his house, he entertaining generally with elegance. . . ." The general was a self-made aristocrat in an age of aristocracy, and he was accustomed to living like one.

Line officers out in Jockey Hollow diverted themselves with visits to nearby kin or friends and on sleighing parties with local girls and dances in the village. On one occasion a captain complained only half heartedly, "three nights till after two o'clock have they made us keep it up."

Enlisted men, who didn't have officer freedom and seldom had the clothes or means to leave camp, had to content themselves with an occasional public celebration, such as the St. Patrick's Day salute to Ireland, when a Pennsylvania officer, in spite of outrageous cost, managed to buy a hogshead of rum for his men.

The severity of the 1779-80 winter did not let up for months. In February, Baron Johann de Kalb, a foreign volunteer, wrote to a friend that the "ink freezes in my pen, while I am sitting close to the fire." The relief furnished to the army by Washington's levy faded. Money continued to be so sparse that for a time the army could not forward military dispatches for lack of cash to pay express riders.

Despite the winter's severity, the work of the army had to go on. Firewood and water had to be fetched. The rations that did get through had to be distributed and cooked and the few remaining animals cared for. Tailors had to patch together threadbare clothing, and cobblers had to fashion covering for bare feet. Company streets and parade grounds had to be as clear as possible. Order and discipline had to be maintained. Training continued under the eyes of the drillmasters Baron von Steuben had created the year before. Outpost and patrol and sentry duties stood—the enemy made a number of jabs at the army's perimeter, and on at least one occasion Washington mounted an assault on the British.

With the "Cold backward Spring" of 1780, a Congressional committee came to inspect the army. It found that the commissaries could barely feed the troops from day to day and that the men had not been paid in five months. It found the army critically short of horses and equipage and without forage for the animals on hand. It reported the army destitute of money and with "not even the shadow of Credit left." Few of the recruits ordered up by Congress had arrived. Finally, the committee, more perceptively than it could have imagined, predicted, "The patience of the soldiery who have endured every degree of conceivable hardship and borne it with fortitude and perseverance . . . is on the point of being exhausted."

On the day of the committee report, almost as a capstone to Washington's travails, the army's perseverence indeed exhausted itself, and for a brief moment mutiny threatened to rend its thin remaining fabric. After roaming the parade ground "growling like sorehead dogs," Private Martin's regiment, without food for several days, threatened to go out into the country and procure some for itself. Following a heated exchange between officers and men at evening roll call, the 8th Connecticut endeavored to induce two other regiments to join it in rebellion. After a confrontation with several officers, during which one was slightly roughed up, tempers cooled, and the mutiny died, for, said Joseph Martin, "We were unwilling to desert the cause of our country, when in distress . . . we knew her cause involved our own."

The army did not mutiny. It survived. When the 1780 campaign finally opened in June, the gaunt veterans who marched from Jockey Hollow to various fronts were determined and ready to fight once again for the cause to which they had pledged themselves. The quiet glory of the Morristown winter is that these forefathers, unpaid, freezing, and hungry, shouldered through the cruelest season of the whole 18th century because they believed that their country's cause was their own.

The principal sites of the Continental Army's winter at Morristown—Washington's headquarters and the great expanse of Jockey Hollow—are carefully preserved today under the custodianship of the National Park Service. The visitor can walk through the handsome Ford Mansion and imagine it alive with the bustling of Washington and his aides as they struggled with the daily problem of supply, recruitment, desertions, punishments, prisoner exchange, funding, citizens' complaints, and all the myriad other matters that filled their days. Perhaps standing in a corner of the great hall, the visitor can picture briefly the general, his officers, and their ladies in a graceful evening dance to break the monotony of the gray winter.

A few miles away is Jockey Hollow. Purposely kept free of heroic monuments, it is a place where the visitor can, in the words of historian Thomas B. Adams, "walk about in history and see what it has to say." The forest has returned. On a snow-filled winter's day, Jockey Hollow appears largely as it did to campaign-weary, freezing and hungry soldiers who first entered it in the cold of December 1779.

Pause in these woods and let the axmen of the mind's eye hew down oak and walnut and chestnut and build a snowbound "log house city" as far as the eye can see. People it with ragged, cold, and hungry men, standing sentry, carrying water or firewood, drilling in the icy wind. Enter one of the huts and crowd with its inhabitants to the chimneyplace. And hear the wind.

"Passion and truth are the life of memorials," historian Adams declares. Morristown as presented in this volume and awaiting the visitor is a memorial of passion and truth.

Part 2

A War of Posts

The Morristown Encampments and the American Revolution
By Russell B. Wesley

In deliberating on this Question it was impossible to forget, that History, our own experience, the advice of our ablest Friends in Europe, the fears of the Enemy, and even the Declarations of Congress demonstrate, that on our Side the War should be defensive. It has even been called a War of Posts. That we should on all Occasions avoid a general Action, or put anything to the Risque, unless compelled by a necessity, into which we ought never to be drawn.

Gen. George Washington,
September 8, 1776

The 1777 Encampment

Drums were used in the Revolution to provide cadence on marches and transmit orders to troops in camp and battle. Most 18th-century drums, like the reproduction side drum shown above, were undecorated.

The bleak, neighboring hilltops were covered with snow when the Continental Army shuffled wearily, Indian-file, into Morristown on Twelfth Night—the 6th of January—1777. That the army was on the road in the winter months, and especially that soldiers should march while civilians were celebrating, suggested how hard the war had gone for the patriot cause. Twelfth Night was, among other festivities, a customary time for weddings. George Washington himself had married Martha Custis on January 6, 18 years before. To make war in this season violated the traditional retreat of 18th-century armies into the warmth of winter quarters. Yet by campaigning when other armies rested, and by interrupting the Christmas ceremonials of their enemies, Washington's Continentals capitalized on their own weakness to wring from British self-assurance the first dramatic triumphs of a desperate cause in need of all the triumphs it could get.

On Christmas Day itself, Washington had led his army across the ice-strewn Delaware River from Pennsylvania into British-occupied New Jersey. The next morning, at dawn of Boxing Day, his troops surprised the sleeping Hessian garrison of Trenton, killing 22, wounding 84, and capturing 918 of a force of about 1,200. Leading his little army of 2,400 back into Pennsylvania before superior numbers of British reinforcements could catch him, Washington nevertheless boldly returned to New Jersey two days before the New Year to strike at another enemy outpost. Narrowly evading Charles Cornwallis' force of perhaps 5,000 at Trenton on the day after New Year's, and leaving about 400 men to face Cornwallis as a rear guard, Washington with about 4,600 Continentals and militia fell upon three British regiments, some 1,200 men, at Princeton

on January 3 and drove them from Nassau Hall and the town.

Washington would have liked to complete the holiday observances by pushing on from Princeton to the British stores and magazines at New Brunswick—where, he later learned to his regret, he could also have snatched up the British military war chest of £70,000. With "six or seven hundred fresh troops, upon a forced march," he believed he could have done it. But by evening of January 3 his men had been under arms for 40 hours, without time to rest or to cook a warm meal against winter's cold. They had marched 16 miles the night before and then fought the battle of Princeton, and some were already dropping asleep by the road. Another important reason for breaking off combat was that Cornwallis, hearing the rumble of the Princeton guns, had come pounding up the road from Trenton to ground the elusive fox whose stratagems had so far frustrated him. Cornwallis' vanguard entered Princeton as Washington's rearguard was leaving.

Past Kingston, Washington's army took the road that forked left along the Millstone River through Rocky Hill to Somerset Courthouse, the present town of Millstone. There the men halted for the night, falling on the ground without blankets, because at Kingston Cornwallis had chosen the wrong fork and marched toward New Brunswick, away from the Americans. Convinced of Washington's consummate craftiness, Cornwallis believed New Brunswick must still be the rebel leader's objective, by some devious route. In fact, Washington had held council with his principal lieutenants on horseback at Kingston, and they agreed, Washington acquiescing reluctantly, that the army should seek rest at Morristown, where three regiments of New England troops were already stationed. On January 4, Washington's regiments pushed on to Pluckemin. There they waited for two days while stragglers caught up before tramping on to the seat of Morris County.

Washington did not propose to stay at Morristown for long. To Maj. Gen. Philip Schuyler he wrote:

"The Enemy, by [our] *two lucky Strokes at Trenton and Princeton, have been obliged to abandon every part of Jersey, except Brunswick and Amboy and the small tract of Country between them, which is so intirely exhausted of Supplies of every kind, that I hope, by preventing them from sending their foraging Parties to any great distance, to reduce them to the utmost distress, in the course of this Winter."*

Similarly, he wrote Gov. Nicholas Cooke of Rhode Island:

"You must be sensible the Season is fast approaching, when a new Campaign will open; nay, the former is not yet closed, neither do I intend it shall, unless the Enemy quits the Jerseys. It is of the last importance to the interest of America, that the New Regiments be speedily levied. It will give me an opportunity, in the fore part of the Campaign, before the Enemy can Collect their force, or receive any reinforcement from home, to give them a fatal Stab. Such a blow, in the forepart of the Season, might terminate the Campaign to great Advantage."

But the regiments were not speedily levied; and while Washington harassed the enemy's foraging parties, his small numbers did not permit him to put enough force into the enterprise to reduce the British to the utmost distress. He delivered no fatal stab. As one week rolled into the next with the recruiting of new regiments by the States still lagging, Washington reconciled himself to the inactivity of winter quarters. He would remain at Morristown.

Morristown ranks with Valley Forge among the places most closely associated in nearly every American's mind with the military campaigns of the Revolution. Yet they were not battlegrounds but winter encampments of the Continental Army. That the names of these campgrounds are more familiar than those of most of the war's battles, suggests much about the character of the Revolution and in fact about 18th-century warfare in general.

To those accustomed to the rapidly moving and almost incessant campaigns of the Second World War, the armies of George Washington's time appear sunk in immobility and leisure. Much of the time, especially from December through June, they clung to their tents and barracks. True, Washington's soldiers were on occasion driven by adversity and their commander's restless temperament to try to break this stagnant pattern, as the Christmas campaign of 1776-77 showed. But the Continental Army was modeled on European armies, and prolonged confinement to its base was so inherent in the nature of an army of the day that the Continentals could not fully break the mold.

An army in the 18th century was a difficult and expensive mechanism for any country to raise and maintain. The European nations of the 1700s, and their American colonies even more so, were agricultural societies without the economic surplus of the industrial age of the 19th and 20th centuries. The able-bodied young men of most families could not afford to take time off from farming to go to war, if the family and indeed the whole nation around it were to subsist. So that farmers could remain in their fields, European mon-

Charles Willson Peale completed this miniature of George Washington in 1777, the year he brought the Continental Army to Morristown for the first time. Washington was then 45 years old and had been Commander in Chief since June 15, 1775, when the Continental Congress sent him to Boston to make an army out of the motley collection of militia then besieging that city. And he had done just that.

The Congress demonstrated its faith in Washington's abilities by granting him extensive powers combining the functions of a regular field commander with the military responsibilities of a colonial governor. His right to make tactical and strategical decisions was virtually unlimited.

Washington's experience during the French and Indian War, most importantly as a brigade commander on Gen. John Forbes' expedition to Fort Duquesne in 1758, had taught him that the key to maintaining an effective military force was discipline, hard work, and attention to administrative detail—all of which he demonstrated at Morristown in 1777 and again in 1779-80.

Strategic Morristown

When Washington first brought his troops to Morristown, it was because he considered it to be the place "best calculated of any in this Quarter, to accommodate and refresh them." He had not planned to stay long, and it was only after circumstances forced him to remain in this small New Jersey community that its advantages as a base for American military operations became fully apparent.

From here Washington could control an extensive agricultural country, cutting off its produce from the British and using it instead to sustain the Continental Army. In the mountainous region northwest of Morristown were many forges and furnaces, such as those at Hibernia, Mount Hope, Ringwood, and Charlottenburg, from which needed iron supplies might be obtained. The position, protected by swamps and mountain ranges to the east, was also difficult for an enemy to attack. In addition to all this, the village was nearly equidistant from Newark, Perth Amboy, and New Brunswick, the main British posts in New Jersey, so that any enemy movement could be met by an American counterblow, either from Washington's own outposts or from the center of his defensive-offensive web at Morristown itself. A position better suited to all the Commander in Chief's purposes, either in the winter of 1777 or in the later 1779-80 encampment period, would have been hard to find.

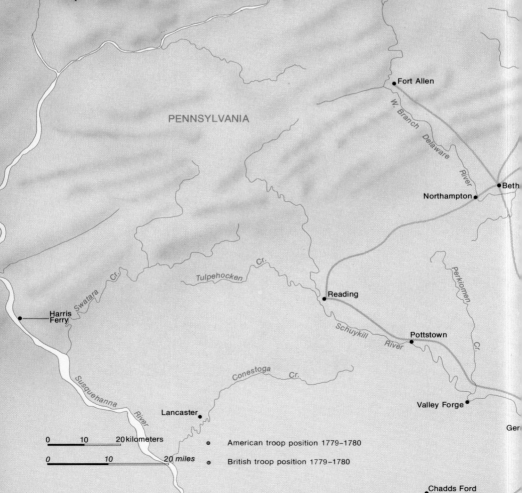

PENNSYLVANIA

Fort Allen

W. Branch Delaware River

Northampton

Beth

Tulpehocken Cr.

Cr.

Perkiomen

Reading

Schuylkill River

Pottstown

Cr.

Swatara Cr.

Harris Ferry

Conestoga Cr.

Valley Forge

Susquehanna River

Lancaster

Ger

| 0 | 10 | 20 kilometers |

| 0 | 10 | 20 miles |

● American troop position 1779–1780

● British troop position 1779–1780

Chadds Ford

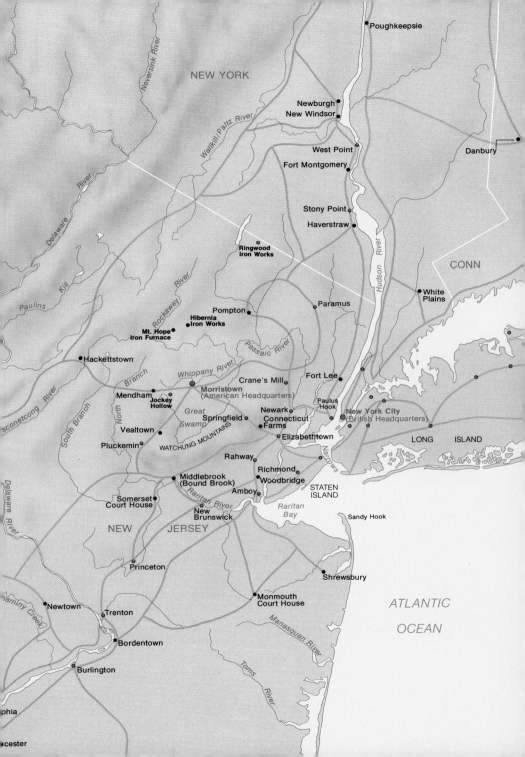

Washington's British Opponents

George III, shown above as Commander in Chief of the British Army in a painting by Benjamin West, usually put army interests above political considerations. He took his duties as Captain-General very seriously and vowed to crush the American "rebellion" by armed might. But the continent proved too vast and the 3,000-mile supply line from Britain too long for his military commanders to deal Washington and his army a decisive blow. Shown above right, top to bottom, are three British generals who tried unsuccessfully to bring Washington's Continentals to bay: Sir William Howe, commander of the British army in America from 1775-78, whose efforts to achieve a political settlement with the patriots hampered his military operations; Sir Henry Clinton, Howe's successor, who possessed solid military virtues and whose attack on Charleston. S.C., in 1780 has been called "the one solid achievement of the war"; and Charles, Lord Cornwallis, Clinton's second in command, a good tactician but bad strategist, whose disobedience of orders ultimately led to the final defeat of Yorktown.

archs like King George III of Great Britain, or the German princes from whom he bought the soldiers loosely called Hessians, recruited their armies from the dregs of society. They enlisted drunkards, criminals, and beggers who did not otherwise contribute to the economy. Even such men as these had to be paid and outfitted with uniforms and equipment. Yet the most diligent of tax collectors could not squeeze from an agricultural population anything like the amounts of money that an efficient internal revenue service can pull from modern industrial societies. Tax collection was difficult. Money to finance armies was hard for the European kings and princes to come by. Therefore, once a kingdom had strained itself to create an army, its rulers did not want the army recklessly drained away in hard campaigns and battlefield casualties. It was better to try to use an army to overawe rivals than actually to fight them.

These pressures circumscribed even George III of Great Britain. Though Britain, as a commercial nation at the center of a worldwide empire, was economically and financially well-off by 18th-century standards, there was still no large treasury surplus to squander on armies. George III's military commander in chief in North America (in 1777, Gen. Sir William Howe) kept his army safely in camp much of the time because he dared not risk it in campaigning unless he felt confident of profitable results. In the cold of winter, the risks were more than ever likely to outweigh the possible advantages of a campaign.

This being so, General Howe was all the more unlikely to allow his subordinate Cornwallis to continue trying to run Washington's army to ground after Princeton, because it might appear to

his government in England that he had already allowed himself to be drawn into too much unconventional winter campaigning, at too high a cost. The 47-year-old Howe, a tall, handsome aristocrat of gracious manners, was exceedingly well connected in England. His elder brothers were George Augustus Howe, a martyred hero of the 1758 battle of Ticonderoga, and Adm. Lord Richard ("Black Dick") Howe, His Majesty's naval commander in chief in North America. The Howes' grandmother had been the mistress of George I and, moreover, the family was powerful among the Whig gentry. Admiral Howe had skillfully assembled a combination of parliamentary hawks and doves to secure for himself and his brother, the general, a commission to negotiate peace with the American rebels. Despite such influence, however, Trenton and Princeton were humiliations too severe for General Howe to afford any repetition of them.

Rather than concentrate his troops in fortified bases at the outset of the winter, the overconfident Howe had scattered garrisons from his main base at New York City all the way across the province of New Jersey. His purpose had been to hold this province, which the revolutionaries had almost abandoned in the autumn of 1776, to British allegiance. But Howe's wintertime tactics had given Washington the opportunity to capture most of the garrison at Trenton, and then, while Howe was calling in his other outposts, to punish the detachment at Princeton. Lest he suffer further embarrassment, Howe intended to confine his troops for the remainder of the winter to New York, except for large outposts of 5,000 each at Amboy and New Brunswick.

There was a yet more fundamental

cause why 18th-century European armies such as Howe's spent so much time in camp, and why the American Revolution after 1777 became, in Washington's phrase, a war of posts, symbolized as much by its campgrounds as its battlefields. For what reason does an army forsake the security of well-guarded bases for the rigors and risks of a campaign? In 20th-century wars, and in fact since the time of the French Revolution and Napoleon, the answer has been simple: an army takes the field and risks its own destruction in order to try to destroy the enemy army in battle and thus bring an end to the war. Elementary as this motive is to us, it was not so evident to 18th-century generals, particularly to William Howe.

In the campaign of 1776, before Washington's Christmas Day descent on Trenton, Howe had several opportunities to destroy the Continental Army. Landing on Staten Island in the summer and then driving Washington off Long Island and Manhattan, out of the New York area and across New Jersey, Howe maintained a superiority over the American forces in quality of troops, as well as in generalship. Beating the amateur and poorly armed Continental Army in one battle after another, he had the Continentals on the ropes three times (on August 27 at Long Island, on September 15 in the retreat from New York City, and on November 16 at Fort Washington) and each time seemed poised to deliver the final punch. But he never delivered it. Howe did not really seem to want to destroy the enemy army.

Occasionally, he said that destroying Washington's army was his objective, but his actions spoke otherwise. In partnership with his brother, General Howe, until September 11, 1776, when the Continental Congress rejected his peace initiatives, hoped to end the American war by offering the rebels the carrot as well as the stick. He believed that because the British army could not patrol North America forever, the only sure means of restoring the colonies to the empire was conciliation. While he believed the rebel army must be defeated often enough to convince the patriots of the futility of revolution, the ruthless destruction of the Continental Army would only harden feelings and make conciliation more difficult.

Besides these immediate considerations, Howe may also have been restrained from swinging a knockout punch by his conceptions of war. The very idea of destroying the enemy army was inconsistent with the assumptions of European generals. Wars in the 18th-century were waged by kings and princes and their hired armies against other kings and princes and their hired armies. Each side aimed to win advantages against the other in territorial gains or through favorable alliances. But neither wanted to overthrow the other altogether, because the destruction of one king might threaten the stability of the whole monarchical system. Rising democratic aspirations among the middle classes were already on the horizon anyway. A sensitive ear could already catch the stirrings of the coming French Revolution. In these circumstances, European wars, not aimed at destroying enemy governments, also did not aim at the destruction of enemy armies. The very conception of the complete overthrow of the enemy army, as the prelude to complete political victory in war, awaited the French Revolution, Napoleon, and the democratization of both governments and war. As an 18th-century general, Howe had never been educated to bestir himself from his bases and go out to destroy the enemy army. Even if he occasionally talked about doing so, he could not break his old habits of thought about the nature of war.

European armies of the time waged wars of maneuver, seeking to occupy strategically important places and hold them as bargaining chips for peace negotiations. So Howe believed in the winter of 1777 that, in spite of setbacks at Trenton and Princeton, he was well on his way to winning the American war. Ensconced in New York, he controlled one of the best harbors in North America, from which his brother's fleet could launch naval and amphibious operations up and down the rebel coast. Since December 8, 1776, Sir Henry Clinton with a British force of 6,000 had occupied Newport, R.I., the excellence of whose harbor had in recent years nourished a flourishing trade. Howe knew that next summer London planned to send another British army toward New York from Canada along the St. Lawrence River-Richelieu River-Lake Champlain-Hudson River route. He expected that army to gain control of this strategic avenue and thus separate the New England hotbed of rebellion from the other, presumably more pliable, colonies. As for his own army, Howe proposed in good time—when the weather improved—to move much of it to Philadelphia. Surely when he seized that city, the largest in the colonies, the rebel capital, and the seat of the Continental Congress, the patriots would be ready to discuss their return to their old loyalties. Meanwhile, controlling the New York City area and Newport, he had no cause to make haste.

George Washington, approaching his 45th birthday, was a Virginia planter and not, like Howe, a professional soldier. Nevertheless, Washington had considerable military experience as a militia officer with the British Army during the French and Indian War. He was tall, erect, and soldierly in his bearing, and enough of an 18th-century soldier in his attitudes that considerations similar to Howe's also helped shape his conduct of the war. His army was also enough a replica of the British army that it was normal to hold it in its camps and quarters during winter in the north.

In fact, whenever suggestions arose that the Continental Army ought to follow some other model than that of the British Army in its organization, strategy, and tactics, Washington rejected them. Particularly, he and the Continental Congress rejected all suggestions that the American Revolution ought to become anything resembling what the 20th century would call a "war of national liberation," and that the revolutionary soldiers ought to become guerrillas—or to use the term of Washington's day, partisans. Had they become partisans, the Continental soldiers might have campaigned in all seasons, continually harassing every exposed enemy outpost or detachment, then fading into the forests for safety while awaiting an opportunity to strike again. As partisans, the revolutionaries would have broken all the usual rules of war, which protected civilians and personal property and even restricted the ways in which enemy soldiers might be assailed, for breaking the rules is the essence of partisan war. In the South, in the Carolinas and Georgia, the Revolution eventually became such a war after the southern Continental Army had been destroyed by British

The Continental Soldier

The Continental soldier won American independence. True, he had help from European allies and British apathy toward the war aided his cause; but it was the Continental soldier—officer as well as enlisted man—who bore the brunt of the campaigns, held fast under nearly impossible conditions, suffered from lack of food, medicine, clothing, shelter, and pay, and in six years of fighting learned to face one of the world's best armies as an equal.

When fighting broke out at Lexington and Concord on April 19, 1775, there were no plans for a national army. But patriot leaders soon realized that they would have to have a regular and efficient army if they wanted to negotiate with Great Britain from a position of strength. Thus Congress created the Continental Army and placed George Washington at its head.

The army's development was painfully slow, but hard campaigns, good training, and good leadership transformed a group of inexperienced youths, partially trained men, and ancient veterans into a tough, cohesive fighting machine that could stand up to British regulars on the field of battle and eventually win a long and difficult war.

The disciplined veteran shown completely uniformed and equipped at right represents an ideal rarely attained in the field. The cartridge box on his right hip holds his ammunition. He is loading a captured "Brown Bess" musket. When properly trained and competently led, he and others like him made formidable foes to the British army.

Musicians, like the drummer shown here, used their instruments to raise morale, provide a cadence for marching, and increase the pomp of ceremonies. But their most important function was to convey orders and signals, which they did far better than the human voice. Musicians traditionally wore the reverse colors of their regiments, making them easier for an officer to spot if he needed to give a signal in an emergency.

A private soldier carried his personal belongings on his back. High-ranking officers often had wagons and trunks, but enlisted men had to use a knapsack, a haversack, or a newly invented combination of the two. Into these packs he stuffed spare items of clothing (if he had them) and his food, eating utensils, paper, pencil, marbles, dice or playing cards, a journal if he kept one, and anything else that he wanted badly enough to be willing to carry it around. This rear view shows how a soldier might have managed all this gear.

action. To Washington, however, partisan warfare seemed too likely to undermine all law and order, the whole social contract, and also seemed beneath the dignity of the patriot cause. Thus, it was Washington's purpose to model the Continental Army on the British Army and to fight the British Army on its own terms.

The Continental Army could not be, and Washington did not want it to be, a precise replica of the British Army. For one thing, its rank and file were recruited differently. As the military embodiment of the American aspiration for liberty, Washington's army was not simply swept up from among the lowest, unproductive classes of the population, as Howe's British and German forces were. Nor were the motives of its soldiers so mercenary. In these respects, Washington was freer than Howe to run risks with his army, including the risks of winter campaigning. If some of Washington's soldiers fell in action or succumbed to harsh weather, their places presumably would be taken by others equally dedicated to liberty, without inordinate expense to the Continental Congress, because American revolutionaries supposedly did not enlist for pay only. As a matter of fact, Congress did not pay on a dependable schedule.

It is easy to exaggerate the differences between the two armies. Just as European farmers or small tradesmen could not afford to abandon their fields or shops for indefinite periods of military service, so American farmers, artisans, and shopkeepers hesitated to leave their livelihoods and go off to war, even in the name of American liberty. Some might do so for a single year, leaving affairs at home in charge of wives or older children. But it was largely because so few solid citizens willingly left home for more than a year that most of the first troops, at the outbreak of the war in 1775, were enlisted to serve only until December 31, 1775. Likewise when the Continental Congress recruited a new army for 1776, enlistments were made for only another one-year term.

At that, it was increasingly only men without family responsibilities or property holdings who came forward to answer new appeals for recruits, young men whose places in life were not yet settled, younger sons, apprentices (sometimes seeking to escape their apprenticeship), indentured servants, day laborers, and (in an army that was racially integrated, despite a hardening American color line) black men. Altogether, in social and economic composition, the Continental Army turned out to be not much different from European armies after all. In fact, when the one-year enlistment term of the 1776 army expired, Congress concluded that the state of the army required a different enlistment policy from that of the perceding two years. The next Continental Army would be recruited for a term of three years or the duration of the war. (Congress was not clear about what would happen if the war should last more than three years.) Considering what sort of men were willing to be recruited at all, Congress decided it might as well try for three years, and avoid having to rebuild the whole army annually. But if the financially struggling United States government could actually find the means to enlist and train such a long-term army, it too would have on its hands an investment not to be risked lightly.

The enlistment and training of such an army was fraught with so many difficulties that Washington was obliged to abandon his thoughts of pursuing the winter campaign "to great Advantage" and instead resolved to stay in winter quarters around Morristown. Washington's crossing of the Delaware on December 25, 1776, and his subsequent victories at Trenton and Princeton are justly famous in history as a turning point in the Revolution. Before these events, the Revolution seemed to have degenerated into a hopeless succession of American defeats. Under the hammer blows of Howe's victories around New York in the summer of 1776 and with the downright flight of Washington across New Jersey in the fall, the Revolutionary army enlisted for 1776 disintegrated. With the Revolutionary cause so palsied, no new enlistments worth mentioning took place in the last weeks of 1776, under Congress' three-year term or any other. Washington's attack on Trenton was a desperate attempt to accomplish something, almost anything, with what remained of the 1776 army, while he still commanded an army. At most, if new enlistments did not come forward, Washington's whole strength after December 31, 1776, would be 1,400 to 1,500 men, all under varying enlistment terms that would soon expire. Washington wrote just before Trenton: "if every nerve is not strain'd to recruit the New Army with all possible expedition, I think the game is pretty near up." The reason Trenton and Princeton represent a turning point is that they restored confidence in the ability of George Washington to hold an army together.

But Washington's surprising victories brought in only barely enough enlistments. On the strength of Trenton, Washington appealed to his veterans to stay in the army for six weeks after December 31, 1776, in return for a bounty of $10 plus regular pay. Some 1,200 to 1,400 New England soldiers agreed, enough to make Princeton possible, but of these only 800 remained around Morristown by January 19. Ten days later, Washington warned the Continental Congress that he was about to be reduced "to the Situation . . . of scarce having any army at all." Those whom Trenton and Princeton inspired to enlist preferred generally to wait for spring before they translated inspiration into action. The happy reversal of Revolutionary fortunes was not nearly so dramatic at the time as the passage of years has made it seem.

The British claimed they received 3,000 American deserters in the first five months of 1777. No doubt they exaggerated, but Washington remarked on January 31 that he might soon have to detach half the army to bring back the other half. By March 14, Washington still had fewer than 3,000 men in camp, of whom two-thirds were short-term militia mustered into service to "keep up Appearances," as Washington put it, but due to go home at the end of the month. As late as April 12, Washington still lamented: "I wish I could see any prospect of an Army, fit to make proper opposition, formed anywhere." So small was the Continental Army of early 1777, so slow its recruitment, that except for a detachment at Bound Brook in April, the adjutants apparently did not bother to prepare strength returns until May. Considering Washington's customary insistence on accurate records and accounting, this seeming neglect implies chaos.

Washington's strategic position at Morristown, combined with the memory of Trenton and Princeton, discouraged Howe from venturing out of winter quarters. The Appalachian Mountains cross northern New Jersey diagonally from northeast to southwest. The main ridges lie behind Morristown, rising generally west of a line from Suffern through Morristown to Milford. But between Morristown and the British at Amboy and New Brunswick, the First and Second Watchung Mountains formed a barrier to a British advance, or even to British knowledge of the sad condition of the Continental Army.

The barrier is some 30 miles long, reaching from the Raritan River in the south almost to the northern boundary of New Jersey, where the Watchungs merge into the Ramapos. The British in the New York City area could not easily turn such a line. To approach Morristown from the east, if they could make their way through the defiles of the Watchungs, the British would find forbidding swamps flanking the road toward Morristown from Chatham to Bottle Hill, near the site of the present Madison. Even today, the Great Swamp south of the road remains little populated.

Morristown in 1777 consisted of 50 or 60 buildings occupying a high plateau, an outlying shoulder of the Appalachians that drops abruptly to the Whippany River. Other hills enclosed the town to the east and north. Passes through the mountains to the west were negotiable enough for wagons to bring in supplies, and the immediate surrounding area, Morris County, was among the few stoutly Revolutionary sections of New Jersey. Northwest of Morristown, furnaces, forges, and bloomeries could provide iron prod-

Two of Washington's officers who had close associations with the Morristown area were Lt. Col. Alexander Hamilton, above top, and Maj. Gen. William Alexander ("Lord Stirling"). It was here in 1779 that Hamilton, one of Washington's trusted aides, met and courted his wife, Elizabeth Schuyler. General Alexander, who had an elegant home at nearby Basking Ridge, was one of the owners of the Hibernia Iron Works, north of Morristown, which turned out cannon for the patriot forces.

ucts for the army. Seven iron mines clustered around Boonton in the northern part of Morris County. The Hibernia Furnace, of which Gen. Lord Stirling of the Continental Army was an owner, the Long Pond, Ringwood, and Charlottenburg Furnaces, managed by Robert Erskine, "Geographer and Surveyor to the Army of the United States"—Washington's mapmaker—and other furnaces in Morris and Sussex Counties cast a few guns during the war, but mainly they supplied the army with ammunition and smaller iron implements.

Because the new regiments were raised slowly, Washington had to rely on the defensive advantages of the Morristown area to help conceal his weakness. Usually he preferred to use the short-term militia rather than his Continentals for outpost duties, in foraging expeditions, and to harry enemy foraging and reconnaissance parties. Generally undependable in battle or garrison, the militia could be useful in active, irregular work. But the Continentals were so few from mid-January until April 1777 that the commander in chief interspersed the militia among them to mask their scarcity. Elias Boudinot, a wealthy New Jersey lawyer who spent much of the winter in Morristown and was soon to be commissioned commissary general of prisoners, wrote that to conceal his weakness Washington distributed his soldiers "by 2 & 3 in a House, all along the main Roads around Morris Town for miles, so that the General expectation among the Country people was, that we were 40000 strong." Probably few of "the Country people" or the British were so completely deceived.

For the most part, Morristown itself sheltered only Washington's headquarters staff and guards, and a few senior officers. As many officers as could be spared returned to their home States to help with the recruiting. Clusters of troops guarded the main approaches to Morristown. Maj. Gen. John Sullivan of New Hampshire commanded a detachment at Chatham astride the passage through the Watchungs from the east, while another detachment lay at the present New Providence south of Chatham. Maj. Gen. Nathanael Greene of Rhode Island and Stirling of New Jersey had brigades at Basking Ridge, guarding the route around the southern flank of the Watchungs. Greene, Washington's most capable subordinate whether strategy or logistics were at issue, was sent to Philadelphia in March to deal with Congress about supply, promotions and other administrative problems.

In front of the Watchungs, Maj. Gen. Benjamin Lincoln (whose commission was in the Massachusetts militia until February 19, in the Continental Army thereafter) commanded a force at Bound Brook. He had 2,163 officers and men present and fit for duty when in April his force became the first in the army to resume submitting monthly returns. To Lincoln's right, Brig. Gen. Philemon Dickinson of the New Jersey militia commanded at Somerset Courthouse, and Maj. Gen. Israel Putnam of Massachusetts had a detachment at Princeton. To Lincoln's left, one of Stirling's regiments was advanced across the Watchungs to Quibbletown (modern New Market) and Brig. Gen. William Maxwell, whose home was in Sussex County in northern New Jersey, was posted at Elizabethtown, Newark, and Springfield—almost on the doorstep of the enemy. When a British foraging expedition, perhaps as strong as 4,000, emerged from Amboy on February 23, Maxwell with about 1,000

Continentals and militia blocked their path at Rahway Meeting House and provoked and repelled a charge.

If every ill wind blows some good, Washington could take a measure of comfort from the circumstance that his perilously small army was not big enough to overburden the neighboring agricultural economy. Thus his soldiers were able to subsist without antagonizing the local populace. His supply departments were so rudimentary in their organization, and transportation over the primitive roads was so slow and burdensome, that concentrating a sizable Continental force in one place could mean starvation for some of its members and malnourishment for the others, as Valley Forge was to demonstrate one winter later. With relatively few mouths to feed through the winter of 1777, however, foraging parties sent to roam the neighboring countryside supplemented adequately the wagon trains of foodstuffs dispatched erratically by the army's commissary general.

In December, Congress had granted Washington plenary powers to seize "all the Beef, Pork, Flour, Spirituous Liquors &C &C, not necessary for the Subsistence of the Inhabitants." Using these powers to send out foragers risked injury to the Revolutionary loyalty of Morris County and adjacent areas, because the citizens were rarely happy to yield up their provender. Every 18th-century army, even the best organized, had to resort to such practices, with more or less a display toward compensation. Even in Europe, roads were not enough better than in America to permit satisfactory long-distance overland transportation of an army's food. The recent processions of Howe's army through New Jersey, among inhabitants frequently inclined toward

Toryism, demonstrated dramatically how the mere presence of the rough soldiers of an 18th-century army, and their merely inadvertent brutalities apart from the intentional ones involved in impressing foodstuffs and other supplies, could quickly provoke exasperation and attenuate friendship. The British had marched toward the Delaware in late November 1776 amid sympathetic Jerseyans willing enough to affirm their British allegiance in writing. A few weeks later Howe's army retreated from the Delaware with hostility on every hand. Washington did not want the presence of his soldiers to produce a similar perverse effect. Slow recruiting at least offered the small consolation of minimizing the burden on the inhabitants and the disruption of local life. The patriot soldiers managed to avoid antagonizing New Jersey. Still, Postmaster Ebenezer Hazard, traveling through Morristown the following August, remarked that "the Licenciousness of our Troops had damaged the Town a great Deal."

Typical canteens used by Continental soldiers. The wooden one on the left was found in the Jockey Hollow encampment area; the tin one on the right is a reproduction based on a British pattern.

Both Morristown and Morris County were named for Lewis Morris, the first governor of New Jersey. The town had originated about 1710, under the name New Hanover, as a settlement of pioneers who crossed the Watchung Mountains in response to news of the iron deposits, to work the iron or to serve those who did. The county was organized in 1739, whereupon the township of Morris, formerly New Hanover, was promptly incorporated as its seat. By 1777, though the iron industry had enjoyed a modest if uneven prosperity and the nearby valleys were reasonably fertile, Morristown still had only some 250 inhabitants, largely of New England background.

The town centered on the green, as does today's much larger Morristown. In 1777, the green was also a grazing area for cattle, sheep, and horses. Around it stood the Morris County courthouse and jail, the Presbyterian and Baptist churches, and Jacob Arnold's Tavern, established by Jacob's father, Samuel, about 1740. Mrs. Martha D. Bland of Virginia, the vivacious 25-year-old wife of Col. Theodorick Bland of the 1st Continental Cavalry, who joined her husband at Morristown in April, thought that the church steeples gave the place "a consequential look." On the other hand, she found that except for New York refugees "it is inhabited by the errantist rustics you ever beheld." (Mrs. Bland was something of a snob.) While she felt social life dull except for the activities imported by officers and their wives, and the Morristown girls "formed for the distaff, rather than the tender passions," the town was lively enough before the army's coming that Arnold's Tavern had sprouted an extension with a large public hall for dances. Washington could convene relatively large councils in the hall. According to unsubstantiated tradition, the commander in chief made his headquarters on the second floor of the tavern, with a front room for an office, and another behind it for his living accommodations.

The most pretentious private structure in the town was about a mile northeast of the green along the road to Newark. This was the mansion built recently (1772-74) by Col. Jacob Ford, Jr. Colonel Ford was a grandson of John Ford of Duxbury, Mass., and Woodbridge, N.J., who had acquired 200 acres around Morristown early in the century. The colonel's father, Jacob Ford, Sr., had established an iron foundry and risen to become Morristown's leading citizen—justice of the peace, judge of the courts, landowner, and holder of more than a hundred mortgages. Colonel Ford continued his father's business success. He added a powder mill to supply the Revolutionary military forces and distinguished himself as an enterprising commander of militia defending his section of New Jersey against British encroachment during the campaign of 1776. When the Continental Army arrived, however, the colonel was occupying a sickbed in his mansion. Probably weakened by the exertions of the campaign, he had been seized "with a delerium in his head" while drilling militia on the green on December 31, and now lay near death from pneumonia.

Washington neverthless quartered Capt. Thomas Rodney's Delaware Light Infantry Company of Dover in the Ford Mansion and on January 7 designated them the Commanding Officer's Guard, to replace the 1776 Life Guard, whose members were going home with the rest of the 1776 army. The honorific title and role seem somewhat strange, however, because the en-

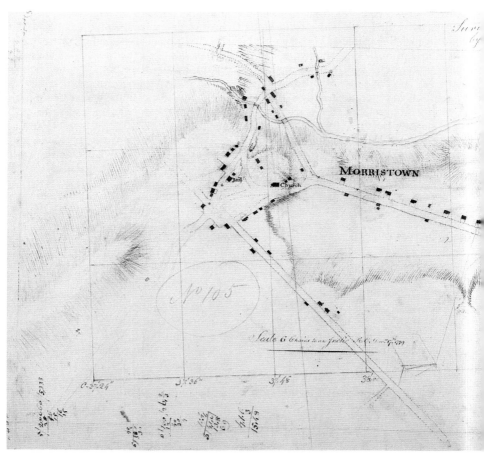

Morristown during the Revolution was called "a very Clever little village, situated in a most beautiful valley at the foot of five mountains." Most of its 250 or so people were farmers, but a few of its families owned and operated nearby ironworks making a valuable contribution to the American war effort. Among the 50 or 60 buildings in Morristown, the most important seem to have been the Arnold Tavern, the Presbyterian and Baptist churches (used as hospitals during the smallpox epidemic of 1777), and the

Morris County Courthouse and Jail, all located on an open "Green" from which streets radiated in several directions. There were also a few sawmills, gristmills, and a powder mill, the last built on the Whippany River in 1776 by Col. Jacob Ford, Jr., commander of the Eastern Battalion, Morris County Militia. This map of Morristown proper was drawn by Col. Robert Erskine, Surveyor-General of the Continental Army, on December 12, 1779. It was made at the request of General Washington, who

was "extremely anxious to have the Roads in front and rear of the Camp accurately surveyed as speedily as possible." The Ford Mansion, perhaps the most elegant residence in Morristown at that time, is located on the bend in the road in the right center portion of the map.

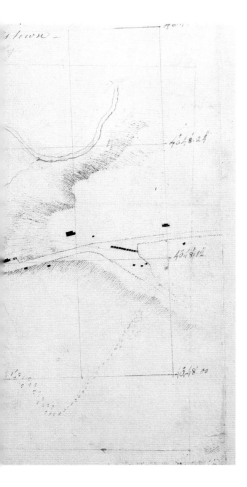

listment of Rodney's company also expired on January 10. Even though they actually remained a few days longer, their principal remaining service was as escort at Colonel Ford's funeral after that gentleman died on the 11th.

The Ford family apparently had no other troops imposed on them immediately, which was just as well, because old Jacob Ford, Sr., aged 73, followed his son in death on January 18. The two widows and Jacob, Jr.'s five children remained.

The deaths that struck the Ford mansion would probably have occurred no matter where Washington had chosen to encamp his army, but the presence of the troops did have one evident and conspicuous impact upon the civilian population of the neighborhood— the introduction of smallpox.

Smallpox was a scourge whose toll in lives and disfigurement pervaded the 18th century. Washington himself bore its scars on his face. It was not until 1796 that Edward Jenner in England conducted the first vaccination with cowpox vesicles. Armies with their congestion and, typically, indifferent sanitation provided an especially hospitable breeding ground for the disease. Smallpox had already ruined one American army, the Revolutionary force that retreated from Canada in 1776. By December 22, 1776, on the eve of Trenton, Washington's army had almost one-third of its privates sick and unfit for duty, and smallpox was among the causes, along with assorted fluxes and fevers. As soon as going into camp around Morristown afforded the necessary leisure, Washington had Dr. Nathaniel Bond begin a mass inoculation of all soldiers not already immunized by the disease. Inoculation involved infecting the pa-

Washington at Morristown

During each of the two winters the Continental Army spent at Morristown, Washington maintained his headquarters in two very different types of buildings. The first of these was the Arnold Tavern (shown above in an 1891 engraving), which faced the village green and which Washington occupied on January 6, 1777. It was owned and operated by Jacob Arnold, onetime sheriff of Morris County and, in 1777, Captain of the Morris "Light Horse" troop of cavalry.

The three-story tavern, with its broad central hall and spacious winding stairway, easily accommodated Washington's corps of aides and secretaries and the endless stream of men who came to see him on business or military matters. Washington occupied the two rooms over the barroom in the north end of the building, using the front room as an office and the adjoining room as sleeping quarters. It was in these

cramped two rooms that he wrestled with the perplexing problems of how to feed and clothe his hungry and ragged men and how to protect them from the scourge of smallpox that threatened to devastate the army—problems that must be solved if the war was to go on.

From December 1, 1779, to June 23, 1780, during the second Morristown encampment, Washington lived and made his headquarters in a comparatively new two-story house (above right), which had been completed about 1774 on the outskirts of town by Col. Jacob Ford, Jr., wealthy landowner and ironmaster and colonel in the New Jersey militia. Considered the finest house in Morristown, it had served for a brief period in 1777 as quarters for the Delaware Light Infantry commanded by Capt. Thomas Rodney. During the 1779-80 encampment, all but two of its eight rooms were occupied by Washing-

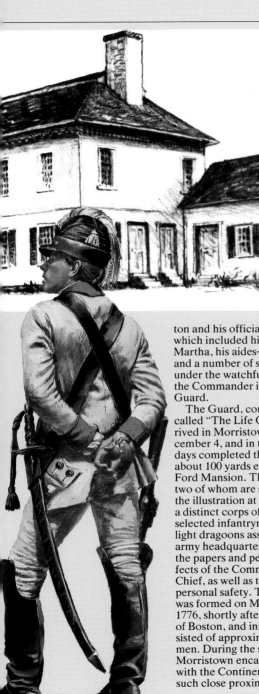

ton and his official family, which included his wife, Martha, his aides-de-camp, and a number of servants, all under the watchful eyes of the Commander in Chief's Guard.

The Guard, commonly called "The Life Guard," arrived in Morristown on December 4, and in the next few days completed their huts about 100 yards east of the Ford Mansion. These men, two of whom are shown in the illustration at left, formed a distinct corps of carefully selected infantrymen and light dragoons assigned to army headquarters to protect the papers and personal effects of the Commander in Chief, as well as to insure his personal safety. The Guard was formed on March 12, 1776, shortly after the siege of Boston, and initially consisted of approximately 180 men. During the second Morristown encampment, with the Continental Army in such close proximity to the British in New York City, the Guard was increased to 250 men. It was reduced to its original 180 members the following spring, and early in 1783, the last year of its service, it contained only 64 noncommissioned officers and privates.

Despite vague and sometimes contradictory information on its composition, the Life Guard seems to have been composed of native-born Americans, five feet nine inches to five feet ten inches tall. During 1777-78 its members appear to have been primarily Virginians, along with a few Marylanders. After 1778, however, men seem to have been selected from throughout the army, an attempt being made to have at least one representative from each of the States furnishing troops to Washington's forces. The Guard usually carried muskets and occasionally sidearms. It was disbanded in June 1783, when the war was almost over.

tient with a mild form of smallpox to generate immunity against a more severe attack. Compared with the later practice of vaccination with the cowpox, it was a decidedly dangerous means of creating immunity, but the only one available. It also temporarily incapacitated even those it otherwise spared.

For this reason, the inoculation of the army had to be accomplished by dividing the force into a number of groups, inoculated at intervals of five to six days, to keep enough reasonably fit men in the ranks. Because of the perils, inoculation also proceeded secretly at first. At inoculation centers in private houses, guards watched over the recuperating recipients of the doctors' ministrations to ensure they did not venture out to spread the infection. Protecting the army seemed to require, nevertheless, the inoculation of civilians throughout the Morristown area. Whether introduced through the dangers of the inoculation or by the army itself, smallpox struck the area hard. The Morristown Presbyterian Church recorded 68 deaths in its congregation alone in 1777. Not all of these deaths fell among the 250 citizens of the town proper, but comparing the number of deaths with the size of the population nevertheless underlines quickly the ravages of 18th-century epidemics, staggeringly out of proportion to anything known in the developed nations of our own time.

Because the army had almost abandoned record keeping during the winter of 1777, the smallpox toll is unknown. As late as March 14, the inoculation program itself had incapacitated about 1,000 soldiers, while perhaps 2,000 stood ready for duty. Still, by military standards the spring of 1777 was a fairly happy time for the

Revolution, because Howe prolonged his idleness, and in May recruits at last began to enter the camps.

Between July 5 and November 30, 1776, the Continental Congress had authorized an army of 92 infantry regiments, amounting to 66,803 officers and men. In the crisis atmosphere of the end of December, on the day after Trenton when Howe's departure from the line of the Delaware was not yet known, Congress voted an additional 16 infantry regiments with 11,748 officers and men, plus three battalions of artillery and 3,000 cavalry. The authorized army for 1777 would have amounted to 117 regiments with 82,475 officers and men. Though the population of the 13 rebellious States was more than 2½ million, the country's internal political divisions, backward economy, and precarious finances condemned the authorized army to remain merely a dream. Washington had to count himself lucky when by May recruiting at last brought him something over a tenth of the numbers voted by Congress. On May 21 the army around Morristown had 38 understrength infantry regiments and two detachments averaging about 250 men each, for a total of 10,003 officers and men, of which 7,363 officers and men were present and fit for duty. This army was the belated dividend of Trenton and Princeton—and also of bounty payments offered by some of the States, even though the States sometimes undercut themselves by offering similar bounties for mere stay-at-home service in the militia.

This modest recruiting success was enough to raise the specter of famine, and Washington soon had to think about moving on as the alternative to starvation. Meanwhile, his officers began training the new troops, an en-

Representative longarm weapons of the American Revolution: the "Brown Bess," right, the mainstay of both American and British armies early in the war, and the .69-calibre French musket, which became the pattern for American muskets after the war.

deavor whose multiple difficulties offered one of the many arguments against the risks of movement. The armies of the day did not have to be trained to use anything resembling the elaborate weaponry of the 20th-century army. But to meet a well disciplined army such as General Howe's, with the limited numbers to which Washington had to resign himself, and to have a chance of winning the encounters, nevertheless required careful training of a different type: the conditioning of the Continental battalions so they could maneuver across a battlefield under fire as though on a parade ground, and hold their formations unbroken against the shock of bristling bayonets delivered all in line.

Except for light guns, the artillery of the day moved cumbersomely. Artillery served best in defending or battering fixed fortifications. The British brought little cavalry to America, and Washington was slow to try to develop a Continental cavalry arm. Thus the combat of the Revolution in the North resolved itself mainly into infantry fighting. Because the smoothbore muskets of the infantry had an extremely short range—200 or 250 yards at most, but with such little accuracy that it took a good man to hit a barn door at more than 50 yards—the crucial test of the infantry battle was not the exchange of musket volleys but the close-quarter fight with bayonets. On an open battlefield, the British were sure to advance in long lines shoulder to shoulder, each battalion usually two or three ranks deep. As their lines came within range of the American position, they would pause to deliver a volley with their Brown Bess muskets, which would strike down at least a few of the Revolutionaries and, unless the Continentals had received good train-

The British Redcoat

When the Revolutionary War began, Britain's army probably totaled not much above 50,000 men fit for service, far fewer than existed on paper. Because garrison forces were needed for England and elsewhere in the Empire, only part of the army could be spared for North America, and not all of it could be used against the patriot forces because of the need to maintain garrisons in East and West Florida and in Canada. Had it not been for the hiring of "Hessian" mercenaries, Britain would not have had sufficient men to keep the field against the American armies.

Even so, the British army was as good as any in the world, and might have been even better had its ranks been filled by the best of British youth. But service in His Majesty's regiments was not an attractive profession. Pay was low, discipline severe, and promotion from the ranks almost unknown. As a result, many a country boy plied with liquor at a tavern by a smooth-talking ensign or sergeant woke up to find himself a member of the King's service. Drifters and loafers signed up because they preferred the hard life of the soldier to misery and starvation. Others enlisted to escape punishment for crimes.

As unreliable as the British recruiting system was, it nevertheless brought into the army tough and hardened men who made good soldiers and produced many fine regiments. The redcoats, serving for long periods, became professional and proficient soldiers who, armed with musket and bayonet, proved formidable on both the defensive and the offensive.

Hussar, Queen's Rangers
Originally an infantry regiment, this unit took part in the 1777 Philadelphia campaign, fighting at the Brandywine and Germantown. It returned to New York in 1778

Officer, Royal Artillery
Originally derived from the Train of Artillery, which had formed part of Marlborough's army, the Royal Artillery Regiment was formed in 1716. Units of the regiment served in virtually every post and battle of the war, with the 4th Battalion mostly serving in America. Commanded by Gen. James Pattison.

nd took part in the Battle of
Monmouth Court House. The
egiment, commanded by
Col. John Simcoe, was part
f the New York garrison at
he time of the second
Morristown encampment.

Grenadier, 57th Regiment
*Formed as the 59th Regiment
of Foot in 1755, it was redes-
ignated in 1757. It arrived in
America from Cork, Ireland,
in May 1776, and took part in
the first siege of Charleston.
Subsequently sent on the 1776
New York campaign, it
fought in the Battle of Long
Island on August 27. Under
the command of Col. John
Campbell, it was stationed in
New York until sent to Hali-
fax in September 1783. The
grenadier shown here was a
member of one of the flank
companies of his regiment,
the other being the light infantry. Grenadier and light
infantry companies were
made up of the best soldiers
in the regiment and were frequently detached for particularly important combat
missions.*

ing, contribute to unnerving the rest.

Then the British lines would come onward again. At some point—perhaps not until they saw the whites of their enemies' eyes—the patriots would let go with their own muskets. Many British would fall. But in the disciplined British regiments, the troops would close ranks to fill the empty spaces and keep advancing. The musket not only had a limited range. As a muzzleloader, it was awkward and time-consuming to load. It could not be loaded while lying down undercover. Once a Revolutionary soldier had fired at effective range, the British would likely be upon him before he could fire again. At best he could get off only two effective shots. The very uniforms of the British regulars—the bright red coats, the pipe-clayed crossbelts, the burnished metal of the buckles and gorgets, the mitred hats of the grenadiers—enhanced the fearsome impression of inexorability as their lines marched closer. At last the British bayonets swung down to the charge and their bearers raced the final yards huzzaing. To stand firm against this onslaught was the climactic trial of discipline and training. Too few Continental battalions were ever trained well enough to survive the trial surely.

Of course, Revolutionary soldiers had stood up well when they were protected by strong entrenchments, most famously at Bunker (Breed's) Hill. But to resist the bayonet charge of disciplined British regulars in the open field was a very different proposition. Still less readily did the Continental Army learn to carry the attack itself against the enemy—to deploy in orderly progression on the battlefield from column of march into line of battle for the attack, and then to maintain the linear attack formation across uneven

ground and against the enemy's defensive volleys, to strike him with that unbroken line of bayonets without which a disciplined defender could not be overcome.

The most successful European army of George Washington's day was the Prussian army of Frederick the Great. Though Frederick was an exceptionally skillful strategist, his army's success depended finally on its tactical abilities on the battlefield. Frederick made no major modifications in the basic infantry tactics of the era. He and his army fared so well mainly because his troops were the best disciplined in Europe, his armies built around a core of long-term veterans conditioned to perform against musket-ball and bayonet as though each individual was a mechanical cog in the well-oiled machine that was the regiment.

Washington possessed almost none of the means to transform his recruits into the parts of such a machine. His own experience as a colonial militia officer serving with the British army had given him an intense admiration for the discipline of the redcoats, but he had not served closely enough with the regulars to gain a thorough acquaintance with their tactics and training. The Continental Army acquired a few officers who were veterans of the British regular establishment, but too few to train a whole army, even if the army were small. Unluckily, the most experienced of the few veteran British officers who joined the Revolution chanced to exclude themselves by personality quirks from effective contributions to the Continental Army's training. Maj. Gen. Charles Lee was an eccentric egoist who, though performing useful service in 1775 and 1776, nevertheless eventually antagonized almost everyone. By the time the army went to Morristown, he was a prisoner of the British. Maj. Gen. Horatio Gates, unlike Lee, was admired by many New Englanders, but he was also disliked by many others. He came to be possessed by his jealousy of Washington, and his talents were suited mainly to the business administration of an army, though after 1776 he did little of that. European officers who joined the Continental forces in hopes of finding money, adventure, or fame proved, by and large, a still more inept and quarrelsome lot. By the spring of 1777, they drove Washington to frequent complaints in his letters to Congress from Morristown, and to appeals that no more foreigners be sent him without the most careful scrutiny.

The recruits who slowly found their way to the camps around Morristown thus had to be trained as soldiers by officers who were themselves inexpert in tactics and discipline. Worse, because the heart of any American or British army has always been its sergeants, the enlisted ranks of the new army of 1777 included hardly any non-commissioned officers who could remotely approximate the functions of the modern drill instructor in basic training. The principal means by which Washington and his officers learned how to teach the troops the tactical evolutions of paradeground and battlefield at all was to study books on the subject and then try to apply to the realities of awkward recruits the idealizations of the printed page.

The officers possessed nothing like the official tactical manuals of the modern U.S. Army; but various private authors and publishers had attempted to crystallize military drill from the school of the soldier to the school of the battalion in print. There was Humphrey Bland's *A Treatise of Military Discipline,* published in England in 1727, from which the young Washington had taught himself during the French and Indian War. There was William Windham's *A Plan of Discipline, Composed for the use of the Militia of the County of Norfolk,* published in London in 1760, and appropriate for the Americans because it simplified the tactics of the era for its intended readership of British part-time soldiers. There was the still more simplified *An Easy Plan of Discipline,* by Col. Timothy Pickering of the Massachusetts militia, published at Salem in 1775. There were indeed too many such manuals, at least seven of them in Continental use. Any regiment used whichever one of them its colonel chose. Thus there was no one system of tactics for the entire Continental Army.

Document box, of a type used by general officers to store copies of official correspondence and other important papers.

Still, recruits were coming in, and some of the winter's gloom gave way to a more appropriate springtime mood. A small army is better than no army at all, and from Martha Bland, we have a glimpse of a positively jovial General Washington heartened by the presence since March of his wife Martha: *"Now let us speak* [Mrs. Bland wrote to her sister-in-law Fanny Randolph in Virginia] *of our noble and agreeable commander (for he commands both sexes, one by his excellent skill in military matters, the other by his ability, politeness, and attention). We visit them twice or three times a week by particular invitation. Every day frequently by inclination. He is generally busy in the forenoon, but from dinner till night he is free for all company. His worthy lady seems to be in perfect felicity, while she is by the side of her "Old Man," as she calls him. We often make parties on horseback, the General, his Lady, Miss Livingston* [daughter of Governor William Livingston of New Jersey], *and his aides-de-camp . . . generally at which time General Washington throws off the hero and takes on the chatty agreeable companion. He can be downright impudent sometimes, such impudence, Fanny, as you and I like, and really, I have wished for you often."*

In the busy forenoons, however, the commander labored to share with his subordinates his strategic policy for the remainder of the war, as matured at Morristown by the winter's painfully slow recruiting and the spring's difficult training. To Maj. Gen. Benedict Arnold, who had been sent to defend Rhode Island and who now proposed taking the offensive in that State, Washington wrote restrainingly on March 3:
"I must recall your attention to what I have said before on the Subject of your intended attack. You must be sensible that the most serious ill consequences may and would, probably, result from it in case of failure, and prudence dictates, that it should be cautiously examined in all its lights, before it is attempted. Unless your Strength and Circumstances be such, that you can reasonably promise yourself a moral certainty of succeeding, I would have you by all means to relinquish the undertaking, and confine yourself, in the main, to a defensive opposition."

To Maj. Gen. Philip Schuyler, commanding general of the Northern Army then preparing to resist a possible invasion from Canada, he wrote on March 12:
"It is of the greatest importance to the safety of a Country involved in a defensive War, to endeavour to draw their Troops together at some post at the opening of a Campaign, so central to the theatre of War that they may be sent to the support of any part of the Country, the Enemy may direct their motions against. . . . It is impossible, without knowing the Enemy's intentions, to guard against every sudden incursion, or give protection to all the Inhabitants; some principal object shou'd be had in view, in taking post to cover the most important part of the Country, instead of dividing our force, to give shelter to the whole, to attempt which, cannot fail to give the Enemy an Opportunity of beating us in Detachments, as we are under the necessity of guessing at the Enemy's intentions, and further operations; the great object of attention ought to be, where the most proper place is, to draw our force together, from the Eastward and Westward, to cover the Country, prevent the

Enemy's penetration and annoy them in turn, shou'd our strength be equal to the attempt."

To Brig. Gen. Alexander McDougall, commanding the defenses of the Hudson, on May 1:

"I beg you to take every possible means in your power, to find out the designs of the Enemy and what their plan of operations; do not hesitate at Expence, I know your pains will not be wanting. . . ."

To General Sullivan, now stationed between the enemy and Philadelphia, on May 15:

"It is, I am persuaded, totally unnecessary to say any thing to impress you with an Idea of the necessity of using the greatest Vigilance and precaution; your own reputation, the safety of your Troops, and the good of the Service, are sufficient incitements; but I would advise you to use every possible means to obtain Intelligence of the designs and Movements of the Enemy, that you may act accordingly.

If you find the Enemy's views are turned towards the Delaware, harass and impede their march, as much as possible, disputing every advantageous piece of ground, to give time for the other parts of the Army to come up; but take care to do this in such a manner, as to be able at all times, to secure your retreat to the Hilly Country. If, on the other hand, you perceive their intentions are to penetrate the Country towards Morris Town, or the North [Hudson] River, you are to follow close in their rear and annoy them, as much as possible. In either case, I do not wish that you should hazard a general Engagement; because, a defeat of your whole body which would probably follow, from inequality of numbers wou'd bring on a dispersion and dis-couragement of your Troops; whereas to harass them day and Night by a Number of small parties, under good Officers, disputing at the same time advantageous Passes, (with proper precautions to prevent being Surrounded) would do them more real injury without hazarding the bad Consequences of a defeat and rout."

Puzzled, as these letters suggest, over Howe's intentions and particularly over his dallying in New York so long, Washington himself moved on May 28. Though the British had wasted much good warm spring weather already, he was sure they must resume the war soon, and he believed their most likely move would be toward the Delaware and Philadelphia. Thus he shifted his battalions southward from the Morristown area to the Middlebrook Heights, just north of Bound Brook. Here he was within the protective first range of the Watchungs, but only about 8 miles from New Brunswick, and thus close on the flank of the road to Princeton, Trenton, and Philadelphia.

This late 18th-century portable writing desk is very much like those some officers might have used during one or both Morristown encampments.

Departure And Return

The Continental Army entrenched but fought no battle near Middlebrook. Washington's movement from Morristown instead proved the prelude to yet more puzzling conduct by Howe. On June 12, some 18,000 British soldiers forayed from Amboy to New Brunswick and thence in two columns to Somerset and Middlebrook, hoping to lure Washington into battle. But at those places they entrenched, and Washington could readily surmise they were not yet bound for the Delaware. When the American commander then refused to venture obligingly out of his own entrenchments and yield to Howe every tactical advantage, the British suddenly retreated on June 19. On June 26, a second effort by Howe to entice Washington into a tactical trap also failed, following which the British withdrew to Amboy and then to Staten Island. By June 30 Howe had evacuated New Jersey altogether.

This expenditure of training, discipline, and superior tactical skills to no positive purpose was hardly the way to reconquer the rebellious colonies. Yet Howe's conduct grew more puzzling still. On June 17, 1777, another British army, under Maj. Gen. John Burgoyne, began marching south from Canada via the Richelieu River-Lake Champlain route, and Washington for a time suspected that the explanation for Howe's otherwise strange withdrawal to New York must be his intention to move up the Hudson to meet Burgoyne somewhere in the interior of New York State. Instead, Howe embarked his army on a fleet of some 260 warships and transports, and after lingering inexplicably on shipboard in New York harbor for almost 2 weeks, sailed southward on July 23, evidently leaving Burgoyne in the lurch.

Washington's puzzlement was not

quite over, because the British fleet disappeared from all American observation for a time. A complete absence of coordination between Howe and Burgoyne seemed so unlikely that the Patriot commander suspected an elaborate ruse that would end with Howe eventually sailing up the Hudson after all. So the Continental Army, though it did not return to Morristown, was still marching and countermarching through New Jersey during much of August, ready to move either north to the Hudson or south to wherever Howe might reappear in that direction.

Eventually, on August 21, while the army was encamped along the Little Neshaminy Creek in Pennsylvania, Washington learned from a messenger that on the 14th the British fleet had appeared off the Chesapeake Capes and seemed to be standing in. On the 22d Washington learned further that the British were already well up the bay. The Continental Army started south marching through Philadelphia on August 24, and gave battle to Howe's army along Brandywine Creek on September 11. Washington gave battle despite the deficiencies of his army because he thought he could not abandon the Continental capital without at least an effort to resist. His army lost the battle and the British occupied Philadelphia, while Congress fled westward through Pennsylvania to the town of York beyond the Susquehanna. The British scored yet another victory when Washington attacked their Philadelphia defenses at Germantown on October 4. After this defeat, the Continental Army took shelter behind protective hills again for the long, hard winter at Valley Forge.

The Valley Forge winter of 1777-78 caused the Revolutionary army more suffering than the previous winter around Morristown, because while the army had grown bigger during the warm months of 1777, its logistical services had not. The weather from December 19, 1777, when the army reached Valley Forge, to June 18, 1778, when it began to march away, was not especially severe. But feeding and clothing a force of some 10,000 remained beyond the capacities of Washington's quartermaster and commissary officers and the wagon trains on which they depended to haul supplies. The poignant stories, familiar to every American, of soldiers starving and clad in tatters in the snows of Valley Forge are all too true. Some 1,859 perished of typhus, "putrid fever", and smallpox.

Part of the trouble, too, was that Valley Forge was no Morristown in its capacity to nourish the army from the resources of the immediate vicinity. Like Morristown, Valley Forge was strategically situated. The neighboring hills along the Schuylkill River gave Washington's army command of the routes the British must follow should they attempt to press beyond Philadelphia to Continental munitions and storage depots at the towns of Reading, Lancaster, and Carlisle in the interior of Pennsylvania. Like Morristown, Valley Forge — as its name implies — was in a district of iron mines, furnaces, and forges. But the supply depots were too far away to be of much immediate use in sustaining the army, and unlike Morristown, Valley Forge itself was not a substantial community. It was a rural ironmaking plantation, similar to the plantations of the South, though its product was not agricultural. The owner's house, surrounded by a cluster of storehouses, workers' quarters, and lesser structures pertaining to the busi-

*Three foreign officers who
served with distinction under
Washington (clockwise from
left): Gen. Friedrich von
Steuben, who transformed
the Continental Army into a
more effective fighting
force; Louis le Begue de
Presle Duportail, who rose
to major general and chief
engineer of the American
forces; and the multi-lingual
Chevalier Jean Baptiste de
Ternant, who served as
Steuben's interpreter.*

ness, was all there was. Neither were there food supplies such as a more consequential village would have laid in. The surrounding hills were rugged and wooded. To the north and south of these hills, the Schuylkill Valley between Philadelphia and Reading and the Chester Valley extending west to the Lancaster Valley were among America's most productive agricultural areas. But the fertile lowlands were not close enough, and if the farmers had to haul their foodstuffs any distance, many of them preferred selling to the British for hard cash.

The Valley Forge winter barely missed descending into tragedy unbounded and undiluted. One of its few saving graces proved unexpectedly to be contained in the arrival on February 27, 1778, of yet another European officer, Friedrich Wilhelm Augustus, Baron von Steuben, reputedly a former lieutenant general in the service of Frederick the Great of Prussia. Steuben was almost nothing that he claimed to be. Recently (1764-1775) chamberlain at the petty German court of Hohenzollern-Hechingen, where he had received the title of baron, he had been only a captain in Prussia's service.

Not knowing all these facts, but by now thoroughly suspicious of traveling charlatans, Washington nevertheless allowed Steuben to begin training the Continental troops in a version of European military tactics modified to suit the individualism of the American temperament. In this much-needed work Steuben showed ability approaching genius. Beginning by drilling a model company of 100 men, he went on to display his model as a means of teaching the whole army. With the most meager command of English—except for profanity—he con-

trived to make himself the army's drill sergeant. The entire Continental Army henceforth followed a uniform tactical system. He did not in a few months overcome all the tactical deficiencies of the Continental Army. No one man could have done that. Except for a few formations blessed with uncommonly able leadership, the Continental Army was never able to pit equal numbers against the British army, under equal circumstances of tactical advantage, with equal prospects of success. But Steuben did make a positive difference.

Indirectly as well as directly, Steuben's presence and example encouraged a transformation of the Continental forces into a fair facsimile of an army. Military engineering in the Continental Army could hardly have been expected to match the contemporary European systems of fortifications and entrenched camps associated with Louis XIV's great fortress architect Sebastien le Prestre de Vauban and his disciples. Col. Rufus Putnam, who resigned as Chief Engineer late in 1776, had done creditable work for an engineer who was self-taught. But out of a growing consciousness of American deficiencies Washington was, as the British historian George Otto Trevelyan put it, "in no hurry to replace him either by a native amateur, or by one of those numerous foreigners who, to hear them talk, were as good as anything that had appeared since Archimedes; but whose only ascertained qualifications were that they could not speak English, and stood in urgent need of a salary." By the time the army went to Valley Forge, Congress had nevertheless appointed a foreigner, but one who since arriving in Philadelphia in June 1777 had begun to give evidence that Benjamin Franklin and Silas Deane in Paris had been

Training and Drill

The infantry regiment was the backbone of the Continental Army. Cavalry provided a scouting arm and, late in the war, a quick-striking force. Artillery mainly saw action as individual batteries attached to the infantry. Riflemen were useful for scouting, sniping, and defending fixed positions. But in the open field, where most battles occurred, the musket-armed infantryman was usually the key to victory or defeat. And whether he fought or ran depended in large measure on the training

Above: A sample page and foldout diagram from a reprint edition of General von Steuben's Regulations for the Order and Discipline of the Troops of the United States, *showing one element of platoon drill in the Continental Army. Steuben prepared the original manual during the winter of 1778-79 and it remained in use until 1812. The first edition was published in March 1779 and contained no plates or diagrams. It was called the "Blue Book" from the color of its binding. In the illustration at right, an officer forms a platoon into a unit, two ranks deep, as designed by General Steuben.*

he received at the hands of his officers.

Muzzle-loading muskets firing black powder required a method of training and fighting far different from that imposed by the fast-firing automatic rifles of modern warfare. A man could not load a musket efficiently unless he was standing up, and the slower rate of fire and lack of accuracy made it necessary for him to fight as part of a group. Only a closely formed unit could fill a field of fire with bullets and have the strength to deliver or take a bayonet charge when there was not time enough to reload.

Contrary to popular belief, Continental soldiers did not snipe at the British from behind rocks and trees. They fought in a line of battle, shoulder to shoulder in open fields the same as their opponents did, because it was the most sensible way to use the weapons they had. The only difference in tactics between the two armies was that after 1777 the Americans normally used a battle line of two ranks while the British used three.

The discipline to maintain solid formations under fire came slowly. In the war's early years, orders and drill varied from regiment to regiment, depending upon the training manual most popular with the officers who led them. (The photograph at left shows some of the manuals in use just before and during the early years of the Revolution.) It was not until the winter of 1777-78 at Valley Forge that Gen. Friedrich von Steuben, established a uniform system of discipline and trained the troops in it until they became a truly cohesive unit.

correct in vouching for his engineering capacity. This was Col. (afterwards Brig. Gen.) Louis Le Bègue de Presle Duportail. Duportail's first major assignment was to work on the Delaware River forts below Philadelphia. When he joined the army at Valley Forge, there was hope that another department might begin to grow more professional.

The supply departments needed not so much technical military expertise as simply sound business management. The quartermaster general, Thomas Mifflin, in particular did not provide the most basic direction and cohesion for the transportation service. The failure to organize wagons to carry foodstuffs and other supplies to the army at Valley Forge from granaries that, after all, were not so very distant can fairly be laid at his doorstep, even though he resigned his post shortly before the march to Valley Forge. Why he failed has always been an enigma. He was a successful merchant before the war, and in the winter of 1776-77 he had managed a mighty display of energy in helping organize the militia for the defense of his home State of Pennsylvania. Since then he had quarrelled with Washington—essentially because Washington would not regard Mifflin's Pennsylvania as the sole vital center of the war. Perhaps the quarrel explained Mifflin's laxness and lethargy.

In any event, after drifting through the winter with subordinate quartermasters who perpetuated Mifflin's lack of system, Washington at length persuaded Nathanael Greene to take over the department on February 25, 1778. Greene, like Mifflin a successful private businessman before the war, unlike Mifflin promptly began to apply his managerial talents to the sustenance of the Continental Army. It was unfortunate that Joseph Trumbull of Connecticut, former commissary general of purchases, who had contributed to the successful feeding of the army at Morristown, could not be persuaded to resume his post. He had quarrelled with Congress and thought himself persecuted. His deputy, Jeremiah Wadsworth of Connecticut, who carried on the work and in April 1778 officially became head of the department, was neither so able nor so energetic as Trumbull. But Greene oversaw to the movement of foodstuffs, and good management on his part overcame many defects in the commissariat itself.

Valley Forge was a winter of suffering more heartrending because the suffering was not inevitable. Businesslike administration of the Continental Army could have averted much of the hunger and exposure. Happily, the next great winter encampment—at Morristown in 1779-80—demonstrated at least the partial success of the improvements in both administration and officer professionalism initiated at Valley Forge.

Between the first and second Morristown encampments were two years of stalemate. Howe resigned in late 1777 and was replaced in May 1778 by Gen. Sir Henry Clinton, long his second in command. Clinton was only 38 and had often urged Howe toward greater strategic boldness. His own generalship, however, proved no more audacious than Howe's once he bore the responsibility for victory or defeat in the war. Clinton was also unlucky, arriving at the military summit almost simultaneously with the news that France had chosen to ally herself with the American rebels, obviously as a means of seeking revenge for past defeats in her long imperial rivalry with Great Britain.

The French intervention appeared

to make a concentration of British strength at New York the best possible response to the possible arrival of a French fleet and army in America. Clinton embarked his heavy equipment, invalids, and some 3,000 Loyalist men, women, and children on his ships and on June 16-18 evacuated Philadelphia and marched his army across New Jersey. In the course of the march, on June 28, Washington lashed out against what he thought was a rearguard near Monmouth Courthouse. The British force proved much stronger than a mere rearguard, and a large-scale, fierce, but inconclusive battle raged all day—inconclusive partly because Steuben's training had improved Continental tactics but not decisively so, partly because intense heat (92° or higher) quickly exhausted both armies, and partly because Clinton was more interested in reaching New York than in forcing a clear resolution of the contest at Monmouth.

In July, Clinton settled down in New York City under the protection of the British fleet to await further evidence of the course the French intervention might take. Washington, with 28,638 soldiers, was unable to attack the British in their island fortress without the aid of the French fleet, but occasionally harassed their outposts. For the winter of 1778-79, the American commander did not concentrate his troops in a single encampment but spread his army across a wide arc, from Middlebrook in New Jersey across the Hudson Highlands to Danbury in Connecticut. This arrangement eased the problems of feeding the troops, and the quartermaster service had improved enough under Greene's direction that Washington reported the men were better clothed than they had been at Valley Forge. Still, there was some hunger

and, because of the lack of blankets and hats, some suffering from exposure, although the winter of 1778-79 was among the mildest in memory.

Nevertheless, after spending the summer of 1779 in futile hope of cooperation from the French navy for a stroke against New York, Washington decided to risk a concentration of the bulk of the army again in a single winter cantonment. Many of the troops from the "Eastern States"—New England—stayed at Danbury and West Point. But the regiments of the Middle States and the South were concentrated in New Jersey, against the danger that winter weather might impede a swift junction of dispersed forces, should it be needed. Apparently the strategic location behind swamps and the Watchungs, and the memory of reasonably successful supply in the winter of 1777, lured Washington back to Morristown. He told Congress that it was the most suitable place "compatible with our security which could also supply water and wood for covering and fuel."

Portable iron brazier which, when filled with coals, served a variety of uses, including cooking and helping to heat a room or hut.

The Terrible Winter, 1779-80

Whatever the troubles of early 1777, with the smallpox and painfully slow recruitment of the new army, Washington was not alone in recalling with a certain fondness those earlier months in Morristown just after the turn of fortune at Trenton and Princeton. The leading citizens of Morristown, too, remembered with enough pleasure to look forward to sharing again the society of the general and his officers. "My Pipe of Wine By heavens I must have it, or I am ruined," wrote one of them, Lucas Van Beverhoudt, to his suppliers of spirits on the island of St. Croix. "I have frequently Generall Washington & his brave officers to take a Glass of Madaira with me. It is worth the voyage from St. Croix to see the Almost Godlike Man Washington."

When Beverhoudt wrote this letter on November 22, he was anticipating by just over a week Washington's settling in at Morristown, and his cheerfulness was already at odds with the mood of the troops. For the weather was turning bitterly cold, and men sensed that this year would not bless them with a repetition of the mild winter of the year before. Maj. Gen. Johann de Kalb led the Maryland and Delaware Continentals from the Hudson to Morristown on a march that, he said, "lasted six days and traversed a country almost entirely unpeopled; it proved fatal to many of the soldiers, in consequence of the cold, the bad weather, the horrid roads, the necessity of spending the night in the open air and our want of protection from snow and rain."

A soldier diarist, Nathan Beers, recorded snowfalls on November 16, 18, and 29. It was snowing again—a "very severe storm of hail & snow all day" —when Washington arrived at Morristown on December 1. The troops reached Morristown mainly during the first week of the month, with much snow on the ground and more still falling. Others continued coming in toward mid-month, such as Surgeon James Thacher, who *"marched to Pompton on the 9th, and on the 14th reached this wilderness, about three miles from Morristown. ... The snow on the ground is about two feet deep, and the weather extremely cold; the soldiers are destitute of both tents and blankets, and some of them are actually barefooted and almost naked. Our only defence against the inclemency of the weather consists of brush wood thrown together. Our lodging the last night was on the frozen ground."*

The "wilderness, about four miles from Morristown," was the area called Jockey Hollow, sheltered among hills southwest of the town. Washington had selected the site on November 30, sending Greene forward to lay out orderly campgrounds for the various regiments, whence they could deploy readily for defense. The new Morristown camps would form a line stretching from the center of the Watchungs toward Basking Ridge and the mountains' southern flank. On December 1, Greene wrote to several of the troop commanders: *"The position is fixed upon for hutting the Army a little back of Mr. [Peter] Kembles. The General has made choice of this place in preference to any other, from its interior position. The ground is mountainous and uneven; and therefore will not be so agreeable as I could wish. There is wood I am in hopes sufficient for the purpose of hutting & firing, if it is used properly. There is water in plenty, tho in some places it will be some distance to fetch. The ground I think will be pretty dry; I shall have the whole of it laid off this day; you will therefore order the troops to march immediately; or if you think it more convenient tomorrow morning."*

Eight infantry brigades with 10,799 officers and men marched into the places Greene assigned to them in Jockey Hollow: Brig. Gen. Edward Hand's Brigade (the 4th and 11th Pennsylvania regiments and the 1st and 2d Canadian Regiments, the latter so designated because they were originally recruited in Canada, but now actually made up of men from a number of the rebellious provinces as well as Canadians and other foreigners); Brig. Gen. James Clinton's New York Brigade; the 1st and 2d Maryland Brigades under Brig. Gens. William Smallwood and Mordecai Gist, the latter including the Delaware Regiment; the 1st and 2d Connecticut Brigades under Brig. Gens. Samuel Holden Parsons and Jedediah Huntington; and the 1st and 2d Pennsylvania Brigades under Brig. Gen. William Irvine.

Just to the southeast, on the east slope of the hill called Mount Kemble, camped Brig. Gen. John Stark's Brigade of 1,270 officers and men: the 2d Rhode Island Regiment; Col. Henry Sherburne's Additional Continental Regiment, of Connecticut and Maryland men; Col. Samuel B. Webb's Additional Continental Regiment, mostly from Connecticut; and Col. Henry Jackson's Additional Continental Regiment, mostly from around Boston. Brig. Gen. William Maxwell's New Jersey Brigade with 1,314 soldiers—the three New Jersey regiments and Col. Oliver Spencer's Additional Regiment, mostly raised in New Jersey—took position near the upper Passaic River about a mile southwest of Jockey Hollow, on the north side of Hardscrab-

Jockey Hollow Encampment

Washington's troops arrived at Morristown between the first and last weeks of December 1779 and encamped in two lines below the crest of a mountainous 2,000-acre tract of land known as Jockey Hollow. The eight infantry brigades that occupied the site for the next seven months included the 1st and 2d Maryland Brigades, the 1st and 2d Connecticut Brigades, Hand's Brigade (consisting of Canadian and Pennsylvania regiments), the New York Brigade, the 1st and 2d Pennsylvania Brigades, and Stark's

Brigade of Rhode Island, Connecticut, and Massachusetts infantry. (The inset map at right shows the approximate locations of these brigade campsites.) The New Jersey Brigade settled in further south near the mouth of Indian Graves Brook. In all, from 10,000 to 11,000 men occupied the Jockey Hollow area.

Each brigade at Jockey Hollow occupied a sloping, well-drained hillside area approximately 320 yards long and 100 yards deep. The soldiers' huts were arranged eight to a

row and three or four rows deep for each regiment. (The painting on these pages gives an accurate idea of how these huts were arranged.) Officers' huts were placed higher up the hillsides. All were separated by camp streets of varying width. Altogether there were between 1,000 and 1,200 log structures in Jockey Hollow—truly a "log-house city," as visiting schoolmaster Ebenezer Fitch called the encampment.

Life in the camp was hard and dull. Discipline, which never had been good, deter-

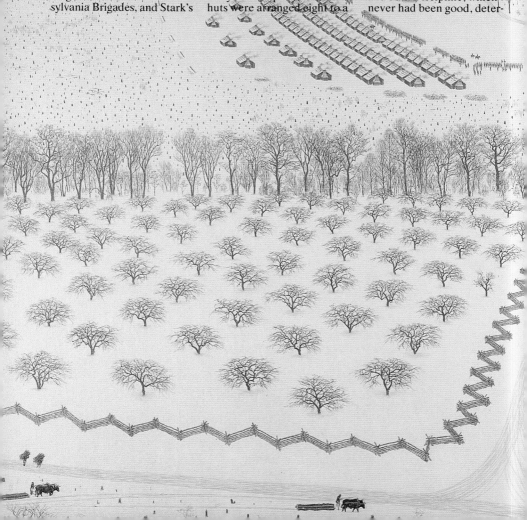

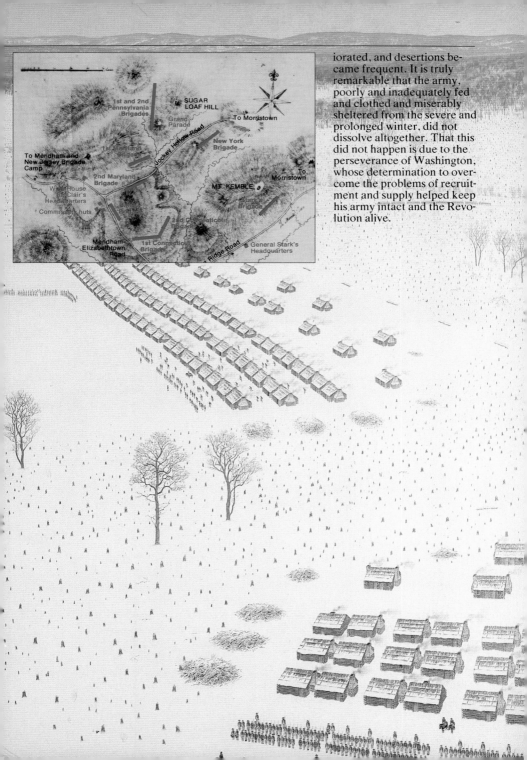

iorated, and desertions became frequent. It is truly remarkable that the army, poorly and inadequately fed and clothed and miserably sheltered from the severe and prolonged winter, did not dissolve altogether. That this did not happen is due to the perseverance of Washington, whose determination to overcome the problems of recruitment and supply helped keep his army intact and the Revolution alive.

1st and 2nd Pennsylvania Brigades

SUGAR LOAF HILL

Grand Parade

To Morristown

Jockey Hollow Road

New York Brigade

To Mendham and New Jersey Brigade Camp

2nd Maryland Brigade

MT. KEMBLE

To Morristown

Wick House St. Clair's Headquarters

Commissary huts

Mendham-Elizabethtown Road

1st Connecticut Brigade

Ridge Road

General Stark's Headquarters

Brig. Gen. Henry Knox (left) was a portly, 25-year-old student of the military arts when he first came to Washington's attention during the Siege of Boston in 1775. A man of great administrative ability and unwavering personal loyalty to the Commander in Chief, Knox made his greatest contribution to the American cause by organizing and training the Corps of Continental Artillery. He succeeded so well that a British officer commented ruefully after the battle of Monmouth in 1778 that "No artillery could be better served than the Americans." The illustration at right shows a typical gun crew in action.

ble Road, which runs between Basking Ridge and Mendham, just west of its modern crossing of U.S. 202. Brig. Gen. Henry Knox established the Artillery Park and encamped his Artillery Brigade about a mile west of Morristown on the Morristown-Mendham road. Greene also allotted space for Brig. Gens. William Woodford's and Peter Muhlenberg's 1st and 2d Virginia Brigades, but these troops had to be hurried southward on December 9 to help meet a growing British threat to South Carolina. The North Carolina regiments had started south in November in response to the same threat.

Including a small force of cavalry— Capt. Henry Bedkin's Independent Corps—the units around Morristown reported a total of 14,628 officers and men, of whom, according to December 1779 returns, 11,053 were present for duty.

On arrival, the men immediately set about building their log huts, and most

of them were out of tents and into the huts by the end of the month. Greene assigned to each brigade a sloping, well-drained hillside about 320 yards long and 100 yards deep, with a parade ground 40 yards deep in front. The soldiers' huts were built eight in a row behind the parade, three or four rows for a regiment. The ridge lines of the roofs ran parallel to the company streets. The company officers' huts stood just behind the soldiers', the field officers' higher up the hillsides. The huts were built of notched logs, with chinks of clay sealing the walls, and boards, slabs, or handsplit shingles covering the roofs. The soldiers' huts followed a standard floor plan, making them about 14 feet wide and 15 or 16 feet long. They were about 6½ feet high at the eaves, had a fireplace and chimney at one end and wooden bunks lining their sides, and were intended to accommodate 12 men each. The officers had larger cabins of more varied

design, usually housing two to four officers and often with two or more fireplaces, chimneys, and doors and a number of windows. The soldiers often cut no windows until the spring. Other types of huts were built as hospitals, guard houses, and orderly rooms. Eventually, some 1,000 to 1,200 log buildings formed a "Log-house city."

Planning beforehand for winter quarters, Greene's organization of the ground, the well-ordered company streets and rows of huts, even the recital of tidy brigade and regimental numerals and designations and the fact that we know so much about their locations—all these features suggest an army well in hand, in apparent confirmation of the improvement in both managerial effectiveness and military professionalism since 1777. The Morristown encampment beginning in December 1779 in fact confirmed improvement, and to that extent the story of the second Morristown encampment is one of success, contrasting with the stark failures of Valley Forge two years earlier. While at least 1,859 soldiers had died during the Valley Forge encampment, only 86 were to die in the winter of 1779-80 at Morristown. The medical and hospital services shared in the growth of professionalism and merit much of the credit for this dramatic contrast in fatalities. But no one who was present at Morristown in the winter of 1779-80 would have been likely to regard his situation optimistically. The harshness of the winter and the lack of adequate winter clothing went far toward overshadowing all the army's improvements. Abetting the winter were difficulties of the Revolution that, though manmade, were beyond the army's control. And behind first appearances, it was the unhappy truth that the army of 1779-80 was far from an adequately organized force, and that two years of effort had only begun to solve the army's problems.

Caring for the Army

During the Morristown encampment, no one was more concerned about the health of his soldiers than George Washington. He believed that every man should have a "healthy spirit in a healthy body" and did what he could to ensure their well-being—not an easy task at a time when both medical knowledge and practice were extremely primitive and characterized by crude instruments and quackery.

The severest winter of the century, an overburdened logistical system, Congressional impotence, and human error seemed to conspire with the primitive medical service to make survival questionable. The Hospital Department, organized by the Continental Congress on July 27, 1775, suffered, as did all the other departments, from a lack of money and supplies. It was also beset by personal strife and constant staff turnover. The prevalence of sickness, together with the primitive methods of treatment, had a very important effect on the morale of the army.

Not only was the medical service primitive, it did not enjoy an especially high priority in the thoughts of most military and political planners. A scarcity of qualified personnel, even by 18th-century standards, was chronic. Many basic items were entirely lacking, and the medical supply was so poor that old tent cloth was used for bandages for wounded soldiers. The congressional committee which investigated the Med-

Trepanning device

Multi-bladed lancet

Amputation

ical Department in May 1780 found it "destitute of those necessaries which are indispensable for the sick." The Department had "neither wine, Tea, sugar, Coffee, Chocolate or spirits," said the committee, "and the army grows more sickly every hour." It urged an immediate supply of those items.

Considering the desperate conditions at the Morristown encampment, it is remarkable that the mortality rate was so low—only 86 men died during the 1779-80 encampment. There is no doubt that the sick and wounded soldiers had to endure a great deal, but the generally hopeful, courageous attitude of the soldiery far outweighed any occurrences of complaints, malingering, or defeatism.

Military hospitals rank as one of the main sources of sickness and death in the Continental Army, due chiefly to contagion caused by overcrowding. Surgeon James Tilton, perhaps the foremost hospital planner of the period, grew alarmed at the high mortality and in 1776 decided to try to alleviate the problem. He discontinued the use of tents and private houses as hospitals, replacing them with specially designed log huts built roughly so that air could freely penetrate the crevices. The mortality from typhus, which caused havoc in the Continental forces during the first two years of the war and was of concern during the 1777 Morristown encampment, diminished markedly, and the general results were so good as to warrant the introduction of the system throughout the army.

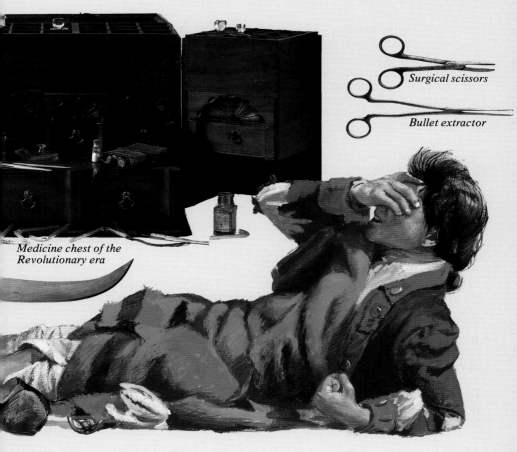

Surgical scissors

Bullet extractor

Medicine chest of the Revolutionary era

The weather was the worst of it. Coming in with snow and sleet, December produced at least seven snowfalls and bitter cold withal. Nathan Beers recorded a "Severe snow storm" on December 28, and as the new month and year of January 1780 began, still worse snow and cold followed. From the 2d to the 4th, icy, piercing winds drove gales of snow before them and tore apart many tents that had not yet been vacated. It was, wrote Dr. James Thacher, "one of the most tremendous snowstorms ever remembered; no man could endure its violence many minutes without danger of his life. . . . Some of the soldiers were actually covered while in their tents and buried like sheep under the snow." When the storm subsided, the snow was from four to six feet deep, obscuring the very traces of the roads by covering the fences that lined them.

Some five more snows followed in January. New York Harbor froze over, along with the Hudson, the Delaware, and their tributary rivers. The British could supply Staten Island by sleigh from New York, and by about mid-month, they could move heavy cannon on trucks across the Hudson to Paulus Hook. Washington feared they might use their sleighs to carry troops up the Hudson and outflank the defenses of the Highlands. In February, it remained "so cold," according to General de Kalb, "that the ink freezes on my pen, while I am sitting close to the fire. The roads are piled with snow until, at some places they are elevated twelve feet above their ordinary level." In March, when Dr. Thacher still reported "an immense body of snow" on the ground—there had been four snowfalls in February, and March brought six more—Washington said that "The oldest people now living in

this country do not remember so hard a Winter as the one now emerging from." "Those who have only been in Valley Forge or Middlebrook during the last two winters, but have not tasted the cruelties of this one," said de Kalb, "know not what it is to suffer."

Certainly the Morristown weather of 1779-80 was the worst of the war, and its fury nearly smothered the progress achieved by a still rudimentary quartermaster administration. In December, General Steuben inspected the New York Brigade and found "the most shocking picture of misery I have ever seen, scarce a man having wherewithal to cover his nakedness in this severe season and a great number very bad with the Itch." After the great storm of the first days of January had blocked the roads and worsened every problem, Quartermaster General Greene lamented: "Poor fellows! They exhibit a picture truly distressing—more than half-naked and two thirds starved." Soldier diaries became litanies reciting again and again the want of provisions.

At the height of the winter storms, men were too cold and too nearly naked to desert or, had they considered it, to plunder the neighboring farmers. As soon as the January gales abated, many did both. Washington thought controlled requisitions greatly preferable to marauding, and in light of the army's desperation he decreed a stern system. He divided New Jersey into 11 districts, set a quota of grain and cattle to be provided by each district, and assigned an officer to each to collect it. The local magistrates were to be called on to help apportion requisitions among individuals. The collecting officers were to scrutinize barns and bins. The stores received would be paid for at some future time when the finances of the United States permitted.

Fortunately, the magistrates cooperated willingly, and an impressive quantity of foodstuffs reached the army. New Jerseyans "more than complied with the requisitions in many instances," said Washington, and by January 27 he could report to Congress that "The situation of the Army for the present is, and has been for some days past, comfortable and easy on the score of provisions." On January 25 the *New-Jersey Journal,* published at nearby Chatham, somewhat extravagantly announced to its readers, "that our army is exuberantly supplied with provisions and every other necessary to make a soldier's life comfortable. The late scarcity they experienced was occasioned by the inclemency of the weather, and large quantities of snow that fell in quick succession upon the back of each other, which made the roads impassable."

As usual with the Revolutionary cause, prosperity did not last. The army ate its way through the requisitions so quickly that by late February, General Greene was again lamenting: "Our provisions are in a manner gone; we have not a ton of hay at command, nor magazines to draw from." As late as May, the diary of Ebenezer Parkman, Jr., was dismally monotonous on the subject: "We are in want of provisions." "Exceeding short as to provisions." "We [are] again very short as to provisions."

The manmade obstacle to army supply that was almost as far beyond the soldiers' control, and almost as devastating, as the weather was the collapse of the Continental currency. Lacking power to tax, and commanding only limited credit, the Continental Congress had no way to finance the war except through issues of paper money. Early in the conflict, reasonably careful limitations of currency issues and reasonably reliable redemption of old notes for new, along with lingering hopes for a prompt return of peace, kept depreciation from getting out of hand. But once the Revolution had dragged on for five years, hopes of imminent victory and thus of redemption of currency in coin approached their end. The buying power of the currency declined at an accelerated pace, Congress felt obliged to issue more and more notes, and in the calamitous climax, the worst winter in generations coincided unhappily with the dollar's fall to depths that made "not worth a Continental" an enduring part of the language. In March 1779, $10 in Continental currency had already sunk to $1 in coin. By the next spring at Morristown, it took $60 Continental to buy $1 in specie. "An ordinary horse," wrote General de Kalb, "is worth $20,000; I say twenty thousand dollars!" "Money is extremely scarce," wrote General Greene, "and worth little when we get it." The army could no longer afford to buy the supplies it needed; the administrative reforms accomplished since Valley Forge flooded away under the tides of inflation.

The Congress had to seek a remedy, but because it had found no better way until now of buying supplies than by printing money, it was doubtful that improvement could be found. The most promising part of the remedial program was the decision on March 18, 1780, to cease issuing unsecured paper money and to begin again with a new, limited issue proclaimed as redeemable in specie after six years, bearing interest at the rate of 5 percent annually. The old currency was to be

Problems of Supply

The winter of 1779-80 has been called the most severe and prolonged of the 18th century. Roads were blocked for days at a time and the delivery of supplies of all sorts to the American army camped at Morristown was correspondingly confused and delayed. It was a time to try not only the souls of the Continental soldiers but their tempers and powers of endurance as well.

Mostly the soldiers lived upon partial rations and sometimes they went without them entirely. Joseph Plumb Martin, who enlisted in 1776 when he was 16 and served in every campaign until the end of the war, recalled with feeling his three "constant companions, Fatigue, Hunger, and Cold." The shortage of clothing was not as chronic as that of provisions, but what little the soldiers received often arrived late and was inferior in quality. Thanks to the magistrates and civilian population of New Jersey, an appeal from Washington brought cheerful, generous, but temporary relief, and saved the army from starvation, disbandment, or such desperate, wholesale

plundering as must have eventually ruined all patriot morale.

The problem lay, as Quartermaster General Nathanael Greene (right) suggested, in the lack of a workable system for the procurement and delivery of army supplies. In 1777 the commissary organization was faulty because lines of authority were not clearly drawn and functions were ill-defined. Flagrant neglect and corruption in the Commissary Department, and negligence in the Transportation Department, hindered both the procurement and delivery efforts. By 1779-80 the commissary system had become more sophisticated and was served by more competent personnel. But because of the depleted financial resources at the disposal of Congress, payment could no longer be made to commissary and quartermaster officials for them to carry out their obligations. Without money, Greene could not gather more than a few days' supply of provisions ahead of consumption, and the army remained half-starved, ragged, and destitute of medical supplies and other necessities.

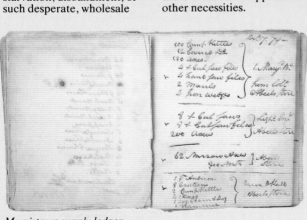

Morristown supply ledger

exchanged for the new at a rate of 40 to 1. To meet the immediate necessities of military supply, however, Congress proposed an arrangement even less calculated than paper money to go on bringing in food and clothing over an extended period of time. There was to be a kind of barter arrangement between the Congress and the States. Each State would be given a quota of quartermaster and commissary stores that it must supply, and its shipments would be credited to the financial quotas already imposed on it by Congress. The States had not been paying these latter quotas reliably. To count goods against money opened the door to endless bookkeeping complexities, disagreements, and debates. Washington soon warned that the first quotas would be inadequate to sustain the army even if they were met. It indicated how well the new system worked that in May hunger drove two Connecticut regiments to mutiny. The mutiny was barely prevented from speading to other troops and then overcome by the patience and persuasiveness of a few of their officers.

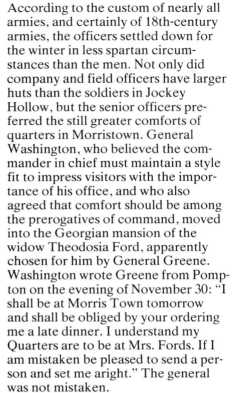

According to the custom of nearly all armies, and certainly of 18th-century armies, the officers settled down for the winter in less spartan circumstances than the men. Not only did company and field officers have larger huts than the soldiers in Jockey Hollow, but the senior officers preferred the still greater comforts of quarters in Morristown. General Washington, who believed the commander in chief must maintain a style fit to impress visitors with the importance of his office, and who also agreed that comfort should be among the prerogatives of command, moved into the Georgian mansion of the widow Theodosia Ford, apparently chosen for him by General Greene. Washington wrote Greene from Pompton on the evening of November 30: "I shall be at Morris Town tomorrow and shall be obliged by your ordering me a late dinner. I understand my Quarters are to be at Mrs. Fords. If I am mistaken be pleased to send a person and set me aright." The general was not mistaken.

The Ford Mansion suited Washington's notions about the dignity of his office, and Mrs. Ford welcomed him as a gracious hostess, bound to the Revolutionary cause by her husband's death through illness contracted in its service. The commander in chief and his aides and servants—his military "family" of 10 to 15 and sometimes more—needed nearly all the space the mansion afforded, two rooms of the four on the first floor, the entire upper floor of five rooms, the kitchen, the cellar, and the stable. Mrs. Ford and her four children, ranging in age now from nearly 8 to 17, retreated into two rooms on the east side of the main hallway on the first floor. On December 31, Mrs. Washington arrived from

Officer's camp lantern.

Mount Vernon.

Gabriel Ford, a boy of 14, was apparently thrilled to be among soldiers and the paraphernalia of war. Years later, in his 80s, he regaled the historian Benson J. Lossing with anecdotes of life with General Washington. Predictably, he stressed the general's courtesy and consideration for the Ford household. Washington, he said, promptly on occupying the house had an inventory made of all articles in it that were appropriated for his use. When he left, one silver tablespoon proved to be missing. Soon afterward Mrs. Ford received a spoon bearing the initials G.W.

Gabriel Ford also remembered a few inconveniences. Washington's Life Guard, grown to about 250 men, built their log huts on a meadow just southeast of the Ford Mansion. Whenever sentries raised an alarm—often, as Ford told Lossing, simply because "some young suitor, who had been *sparking* until a late hour...attempted to pass a sentinel without giving the countersign"—soldiers of the Life Guard would rush into the house, barricade the doors, and generally position themselves with muskets charged and cocked at open windows. Then "both Mrs. Washington and Mrs. Ford were obliged to be in bed, sometimes for hours, with their rooms full of soldiers, and the keen winter air from the open windows piercing through their drawn curtains." But the solicitous commander in chief invariably took time to assure the widow Ford that everything was all right.

If he kept himself in reasonable comfort against the winter's rage in the Ford Mansion, in return Washington gave the Revolutionary cause exceptionally busy labors. If he was somewhat indulgent of his own physical well-being, the commander in chief was indulgent to excess of his officers' requests for furloughs. Too few commissioned officers remained around Morristown to assist him. For many weeks only two brigadier generals were on hand. So Washington had to do too much himself. He had never constructed an adequate staff of officers senior enough in rank to reduce his own burdens by acting with some autonomy. He was his own chief of staff in terms of the day-to-day management of his headquarters, his own chief personnel officer, his own chief of intelligence (coordinating in person an ambitious network of spies), his own chief operations officer, his own planning staff, and despite Greene's considerable help, often his own supply officer.

His aides were young men of great ability, in at least one instance ranging up to brilliance. They were Robert H. Harrison of Maryland and Virginia, at 35 called "the old Secretary"; Tench Tilghman of Maryland and Philadelphia, who combined bravery with business capacity but suffered from a wasting illness contracted at Valley Forge; the brilliant Alexander Hamilton of the West Indies and New York, who had first joined the staff in the earlier Morristown winter, and who now courted and won Gen. Philip Schuyler's daughter Betsy; James McHenry of Ireland and Pennsylvania, a hard worker who was a physician and would one day be Secretary of War; and Richard Kidder Meade of Virginia, a horseman valuable for reconnaissance and courier duties. Capable and loyal as they were, however, these officers were too junior to do more than deliver messages, run other errands, and help with the general's correspondence. They did not give

Washington the support of a genuine military staff.

Thus the general had to deal personally with every issue that reached headquarters, while at the same time, because of the shortage of officers, trying to closely supervise all activity in the field. The weather and the perplexities of supply occupied much of his time. He accomplished the easing of the food supply in January, and when Congress essayed long-term reform of finance and supply, he tactfully pointed out the shortcomings of its proposals and assured reforms as effective as his influence permitted. His attention had to turn again to problems of enlistment, because the three-year terms of the first Morristown winter and spring were about to expire, and the Continental Army was again threatened with disbandment. In this matter, as with supply, he might have been pardoned if he thought—though he never permitted a hint of the thought to escape him—that the efforts of Congress hindered as much as they helped. The legislature persisted in obscuring his estimates of the numbers of new enlistments needed by devising complicated deductions for officers and enlisted men who would agree to serve long terms. The only thing sure about recruiting was that neither Congress nor the States would exert themselves enough to provide Washington with men to do more than continue on the defensive, watching New York and hoping for decisive French aid.

Thus he had gone on since the summer of 1778. The trials of supplying and filling the ranks even of an army barely adequate for defensive waiting suggested that the eventual outcome might well be unhappy. It was all too likely, and the tangible evidence seemed all too plain, that reliance on nothing but patience would produce the gradual deterioration of the Continental Army, while the British would remain in New York and retain their pretensions to sovereignty over the rebellious provinces, until finally the Revolutionaries would have no effective force with which to resist the British, and the cause would die.

The limited operations Washington was able to mount from Morristown gave small hope of a better outcome. Rather, they betrayed his inability to hold alone all the reins of command firmly enough to compensate for absent or ineffectual subordinate officers, and they further reflected the limited improvement of the army since Valley Forge and the coming of Steuben.

When the mercury was near its lowest in January, Washington planned a raid on Staten Island by Lord Stirling. Three thousand troops and a number of cannons were mounted on 500 sleighs for crossing the ice from Elizabethtown Point on the night of January 14-15 to seize the extensive British stores on the island and beat up the defenders. Stirling, though conscientious, unfortunately was neither energetic nor resourceful. The British learned of his approach in time to burrow into their defenses, and the raid was a fiasco. Large numbers of Americans suffered frostbite while lingering on Staten Island for 24 hours without shelter. Dr. Thacher said 500 men were "slightly frozen," while 6 were killed, 16 were captured by the British, and the expedition returned with only a few prisoners and some blankets and minor stores to show for its pains. Worse, New Jersey civilians who accompanied the raid claiming to be militia plundered Staten Island indiscriminately, and the British soon retaliated by stepping up their raids into Essex and Bergen

The French Alliance

France's decision in the winter of 1778 to enter the war as an ally of the United States was crucial to the success of American arms. Yet her entry into the conflict was a protracted affair, and not taken without considerable misgivings, especially on the part of the Bourbon king.

Louis XVI, shown at left in his coronation robes, was only twenty when he inherited the throne in 1774. Though patriotic, conscientious, and possessing "a good working knowledge of the dynastic diplomacy of Europe," he was nevertheless dull and vacillating and had to be convinced by the British defeat at Saratoga in October 1777 and prodded by his ministers to openly back the Americans.

The French had been watching events in America with lively interest from the beginning of the war and, since 1776, had clandestinely furnished the patriots with arms, artillery, ammunition, clothing, shoes, and other supplies. They also provided, with official sanction, a body of young Frenchmen who were impelled by a sincere enthusiasm to join the cause of American liberty. The best known of these was the Marquis de Lafayette (left), who was barely nineteen when he began his love affair with America and who rose to become one of twenty-nine major generals in the Continental Army. Few were more devoted to Washington than this ebullient young Frenchman, and none drew more expressions of affection from the forbidding dignity of the commander in chief. It was Lafayette who brought word to Washington at Morristown on May 10, 1780, of Louis XVI's decision to send more ships and men to aid the Americans.

Counties. On January 25, they surprised and overran some of Washington's outposts, captured more than 60 men, and burned the academy at Newark and the courthouse and meeting house at Elizabethtown. Washington and Stirling tried to recover stolen property and return it to the British authorities, and the local magistrates joined in the effort, but it was too late. Tempers on both sides were already heated, and the war took a new turn toward deeper brutality, of which more must be told later.

On February 2, another enemy raid surprised an American outpost near White Plains, New York, killing 14 men and capturing 76. Some officers clamored for retaliatory raids. But Washington evidently thought that the ineptitude of the defense, the miscarriage on Staten Island, and the hunger and nakedness of his troops in the winter's bitter cold argued against taking the risk. The Revolutionary cause needed help.

On the 19th of April, as the *New-Jersey Journal* described it, there "arrived at Head-Quarters at Morris Town, from Philadelphia, his Excellency Monsieur De La Luzerne, minister plenipotentiary from the court of Versailles, M. Marbois, his Secretary, and a Spanish gentleman of distinction, where they were received with all the honours due to such illustrious personages." It had to be a trial for Washington and a potential embarrassment, considering the condition of the army, to provide a proper welcome and display for the Chevalier de la Luzerne, the Marquis Francois de Barb-Marbois, and their entourage, plus the accompanying Spanish agent, Don Juan de Miralles. Yet the occasion also offered a diversion from the long winter's routine and a cause for re-

kindled hope for the assistance the army so desperately needed.

The negative aspects of the affair turned out worse then anyone could have anticipated. Miralles immediately took sick. For days he tossed feverishly in the guest bedroom of the Ford Mansion across the second-floor hall from Washington's private quarters, until on April 28 he died. Washington and the other available general officers had to serve as chief mourners at the funeral.

Nevertheless, the inexorability of diplomatic courtesy called forth in the meantime a ball and a grand review of four battalions of the army, carefully coached by Steuben, to entertain and edify Luzerne. The review on April 24 seems to have come off at least as well as could be expected. Dr. Thacher thought the "troops exhibited a truly military appearance, and performed the manoeuvres and evolutions in a manner, which afforded much satisfaction to our Commander in Chief. . . . " Washington could also take satisfaction in sensing something of the tenor of the report Luzerne was to send his government, expressing his renewed conviction "of the very great advantage which the republic derives from [Washington's] services." There was still more: Luzerne confided his belief that the Continental Army could indeed expect active French help in the coming campaign of 1780.

On April 27, furthermore, Washington's young French friend—whom he loved almost as a son—the Marquis de Lafayette landed at Boston after a visit to his native country. He brought Washington more cause for grateful tears than the renewal of their paternal and filial affection. On May 10, Lafayette arrived at Morristown with confirmation of what Luzerne had suggested. Six French ships-of-the-line and 6,000 soldiers of the French king were on their way to America. They should arrive off Rhode Island in June. Their instructions called for active participation in joint operations to capture New York City and its garrison. The indispensable help was finally on its way.

The question was whether the Revolutionary cause could survive until the help took hold. At first, Washington hoped the French expedition might arrive in time to be hurried south to aid Charleston, where not only the city but the whole southern Continental Army under General Lincoln appeared hemmed in by the British and on the verge of surrender. But the French were already too late for that. On May 30, Washington learned that on May 12 Charleston had fallen, Lincoln and his army of 5,466 officers and men had surrendered, and the Revolution as an organized military effort was virtually extinguished south of Virginia.

Desertions and the discharge of men enlisted in 1777—to say nothing of the implications of the May 25 mutiny in the Connecticut Line—created immediate peril in the North as well. When he heard the bad news from Charleston, Washington's whole northern army numbered just under 12,000, and was down to half that number around Morristown. To sustain the war until yet another Continental Army might be assembled, Washington on June 2 called for 17,000 militia, to rendezvous by July 15. On June 6, he held a council of war to discuss the employment of his thin battalions. One day later, the Ford Mansion was aroused by a report from Col. Elias Dayton at Elizabethtown that the British were landing in strong force at De Hart's Point nearby and apparently advanc-

ing toward Morristown. British agents and Loyalists kept the army in New York City well apprised of such developments as the Connecticut mutiny, and a British movement at this perilous juncture was not surprising.

Washington began shifting his troops eastward in hopes he could maneuver among the hills and swamps to discourage the enemy without having to fight them. He was among the Short Hills overlooking Springfield the next afternoon when he heard the good news that Colonel Dayton's 3d New Jersey Regiment of Maxwell's Brigade, reinforced by local militia, had put up such a show of stubborn skirmishing in front of the British that at Springfield Bridge on the Rahway River the enemy had turned and retreated. He was now entrenching on high ground northwest of Connecticut Farms (the present town of Union), about 10 miles southeast of Morristown.

Perversely, in the spirit lately regenerated by Stirling's Staten Island foray and with the sort of indifference to their own interests they had indulged in in New Jersey since their first march through the State in 1776, the British had burned the village of Connecticut Farms, including its church, after looting nearly everything they could carry. A British soldier had also fired through a window of the minister's house and killed the minister's wife, Mrs. James Caldwell, while she was sitting with her small children. When word of these events spread among the New Jersey militia and the Continental troops, it did nothing to diminish their resistance.

Lt. Gen. Wilhelm Knyphausen, the senior officer among the British monarch's German mercenaries, was in command at New York City because Sir Henry Clinton had gone with the

South Carolina expedition. Knyphausen led the advance to Springfield.
In his delicate role as a foreigner commanding a British army, he could not
risk a defeat. On the night of June 8,
shielded by a thunderstorm, his troops
pulled back from Connecticut Farms
to De Hart's Point and entrenched
again there. The simplest and most ob-
vious explanation of Knyphausen's
conduct was that, having been warned
by Dayton's resistance that the Revolution was not yet quite so far gone as
he had hoped, he dared run no more
risks and called off his adventure. This
explanation was too simple to satisfy
Washington. Acutely aware that the
Continental Army might indeed be
near the breaking point, Washington
found Knyphausen's most evident motive too faint-hearted to be believed.
He therefore thought the expedition
must be a feint to draw him off guard
in preparation for some additional design yet to unfold. Maj. Henry ("Light
Horse Harry") Lee's cavalry had orders for the Carolinas. Washington re-
voked these orders, summoned other
horsemen, and intensified his reconnaissance and intelligence activities.
He organized a force of 500 under General Hand to harry De Hart's Point,
where the building of a pontoon bridge
to Staten Island persuaded him that
this might be the launching place for
the next enemy move.

Washington's perplexity increased
when he learned on June 20 that six
British ships had sailed up the Hudson
to Verplanck's Point and back again.
This event convinced him he must
watch West Point in the Hudson Highlands as well as New Jersey, and it
became the occasion for moving the
main body of the army away from
Morristown. Leaving General Greene
with about 1,500 Continentals at

The defense of the main bridge over the Rahway River by Col. Israel Angell's 2d Rhode Island Regiment of Stark's brigade was one of the memorable military actions of the Revolutionary War. The 2d Rhode Island had fought in every major battle of the war and had a combat record matched by few American regiments. The regiment's 40-minute stand against veteran British infantry disrupted and helped to turn back Gen. Wilhelm Knyphausen's advance on Morristown in June 1780. The Cannonball House, shown in the painting, still stands near the Rahway River at Springfield.

Springfield—Maxwell's and Stark's brigades of infantry and Lee's cavalry—Washington set out on June 21 with the rest of his army northeast toward Pompton. From Pompton, he could jump either toward the Hudson or back to Morristown, wherever the enemy might threaten.

The explanation for the puzzling British naval excursion on the Hudson lay in the return of General Clinton to New York from the capture of Charleston. At Sandy Hook, Clinton learned much the same information that Washington had recently received about the approach of a French army and fleet toward Rhode Island. In fact, Clinton's source of this information was a traitor in the Continental Army, Maj. Gen. Benedict Arnold, who had gotten it from Washington. Arnold's news led Clinton to prepare to move into Westchester County, New York, to try to place himself between Washington and the French. The ships had made a preliminary foray.

Washington's army marched only one day and 11 miles from Morristown, to Rockaway Bridge, where on the night of June 22-23 the commander in chief learned from Greene that a spy said Clinton would make a move that night. Washington heard cannon shots from the direction of Elizabethtown early in the morning, and at mid-morning of the 23d he received a message from Greene near Springfield that the enemy—Knyphausen with 5,000 infantry—was again advancing on that place. Washington turned his troops southward. Fearing that the British might overrun or outflank Greene, Washington also ordered that the supplies collected at Morristown be removed.

Once more, Dayton's 3d New Jersey offered the first organized resistance to the enemy column as it unrolled from Elizabethtown toward Springfield. While Dayton and some militia made a delaying stand at Connecticut Farms, Greene ordered the planks torn up from Springfield Bridge over the Rahway and from another bridge at Vauxhall, a little over a mile upstream. He left intact two other bridges across a branch of the Rahway just behind the first two, to permit the defenders of the first crossings to retreat. Retreat appeared likely, because even without knowing the exact strength of the British, Greene could nevertheless be sure he was greatly outnumbered. The British came on so quickly this time that Maj. Gen. Philemon Dickinson of the New Jersey militia could not muster more than about 500 men to stand with Greene's 1,000 Continentals, despite the bitterness left by the burning of Connecticut Farms.

Still, Greene intended to fight. He posted his men and Dickinson's behind the main Springfield Bridge. When the British approached Springfield, they divided their force into two columns and sent one of them toward the Vauxhall bridge and around Greene's left. Greene responded by dispatching Dayton's ubiquitous regiment and Lee's cavalry to Vauxhall, where they put up a stubborn resistance but were driven across the Rahway. They had to fall back to attempt another stand at the crossing of the branch stream. Meanwhile the British also opened a heavy attack against the Springfield crossing, where Greene had entrusted the post of honor on the main road to Col. Israel Angell's 2d Rhode Island Regiment of Stark's Brigade. Greene chose well. Though they had recently seemed partially infected by the virus of mutiny prevalent among their Connecticut neighbors, the Rhode Islanders were best known for their stubborn defense of Fort Mercer on the Delaware River during the Philadelphia campaign of 1777. At Springfield they upheld their old reputation. In a 40-minute fight they stood firm against all the cannon shot and musket balls the British could throw at them, until one out of four Rhode Islanders were casualties, whereupon they fell back in good order upon Col. Israel Shreve's 2d New Jersey behind the second bridge.

The British followed without hesitation, for they could easily wade the branch of the Rahway. Shreve's regiment plus some militia continued the fight, but it was now a fighting withdrawal rather than a full-fledged resistance that Shreve conducted. Driven behind the streams, Greene had no intention of attempting a major defense on the unfavorable, level ground between the Rahway and the Short Hills. Rather, with most of his force consolidated, Greene hoped to hold in the hills, though he was not optimistic. On Greene's left, the enemy column that had crossed Vauxhall bridge was still pressing Lee and Dayton so hard that Greene felt obliged to risk detaching Jackson's and Webb's Additional Continental regiments of Stark's Brigade to help against it.

Trying to hurry to the sound of the guns, Washington was able to press the Continental main body only about six miles toward Greene during June 23, but after sunset he received word that the enemy once more had withdrawn. After the Continental reinforcements appeared near Vauxhall, the British column there had marched back to the main force, whereupon the combined enemy columns indulged their taste for arson again—burning all but four of nearly 50 houses in Springfield—and

then marched east to Elizabethtown. "It is certainly difficult if not impossible to ascertain their views," remarked the Continental commander in chief, as perplexed as ever.

In fact, Clinton had intended merely another feint to try to keep Washington away from the French. It was no longer what happened around Morristown but the French reinforcement, as both Washington and Clinton discerned, that would resolve the game.

German-made cavalry pistols and holsters. Most handguns used during the American Revolution were European-made smoothbores which fired a round lead ball by flintlock action. Like the smoothbore muskets, pistols were fairly inaccurate except when fired at extremely close range. Only mounted officers or troopers were permitted to have pistols.

Morristown's War Sputters Out

On June 24, Washington learned that the enemy had withdrawn from New Jersey altogether. Clinton's troops had marched to Staten Island on their pontoon bridge and then pulled up the bridge. With his supplies removed from Morristown, Washington no longer needed to guard the Morris County seat, and he could perceive no immediate objective against which Clinton might strike except the Hudson Highlands. So on the 25th and 26th he moved the whole Continental Army toward the Hudson. Except for detachments, the army never returned to Morristown. But one of the detachments was to write a final chapter symbolic of the mixture of weaknesses and strengths that permeates the history of the Revolutionary army in its Morristown encampments.

In the early winter of 1780-81, the Pennsylvania Line of 10 infantry regiments and one of artillery, commanded by Brig. Gen. Anthony Wayne, returned to Jockey Hollow. They repaired the huts built by Hand's Brigade and the 1st Connecticut Brigade the previous winter and settled in to occupy them for the season.

Wayne feared the Connecticut huts might prove a bad omen, because enough trouble was brewing among his troops to threaten the eruption of a new mutiny. Like most of the 1777 army, the Pennsylvanians had enlisted "for three years or during the war." Unlike some of their contemporaries, they were still in the army, because their State insisted the latter term was the binding one. As the months dragged on dismally, without adequate pay, food, quarters, clothing, blankets, or reinvigorating military success, the soldiers more and more complained that their enlistments properly implied "whichever comes first," and that because more than 3 years had passed, their obligations had expired. In one extremely limited sense, it seemed almost as though the authorities agreed with them after all. By the end of 1780, they had not been paid for over 12 months, not even in paper dollars, the paymaster seeming to think they were out of the army. To go through another winter of freezing and starvation in the face of such neglect from both civilian and military authorities, not to mention their implied contempt of contractual agreements with mere non-commissioned officers and private soldiers, was more than some of the Pennsylvanians were willing to stomach.

Between 9 and 10 p.m. on New Year's Day, 1781, many of the Pennsylvania soldiers emerged from their huts armed and accoutered for battle. They captured several cannons and assembled to march away from their camps. As the officers became aware of what was happening, a tumultuous hour or so followed, while Wayne and other officers attempted through appeals of both discipline and eloquence to disband the assemblage and send the men back to their huts. In the confusion, Capt. Samuel Tolbert and Lt. Francis White were wounded while trying to prevent their men from joining the assemblage, and Capt. Adam Bettin was mortally wounded by a soldier who thought he was shooting a different officer. (The site of the Bettin Oak, under which the captain is said to have been buried, remains a landmark in Jockey Hollow.) A soldier was killed accidentally by another soldier. There may have been additional casualties that went unrecorded, but on the whole the violence was limited, considering that a full-blown mutiny had broken out.

Wayne and the officers soon had to admit that they had a mutiny on their hands. They had predicted that the discontent of their troops might lead to some such eruption, and Wayne had appealed without success to the Pennsylvania government for redress of the soldiers' grievances. But none of that foresight was of much help to the officers now. Not only would the men accept no entreaties to disband, the mutineers forced reluctant troops to join them, bringing in the 2d Regiment, for example, at the point of the bayonet and threatening the 5th and 9th Regiments with artillery until they also joined in. The mutineers stole officers' horses to move the cannons and pillaged regimental supplies.

They were likely to seize any horse they could, in fact, and thus arose the legend of Temperance Wick. Much of the Jockey Hollow encampment was on the property of Henry Wick, who had died of pleurisy on December 21. On New Year's Day, his wife was also sick, and his daughter Temperance, called Tempe, was on her way home on horseback from summoning a physician when she met some mutineers who tried to take her white horse. According to the legend, she pleaded with them to let her ride it home before she yielded it. Then she galloped away to lead it straight through the kitchen and into her bedroom, where she supposedly hid it for several days.

So prolonged a confinement would not have been necessary, for most of the mutineers were gone before midnight. To Wayne's entreaties they had replied with respectful demeanor but said that their officers could not remedy their grievances. Their business was with Congress and the State government in Philadelphia. About 11 p.m., some 1,500 of the approximately 2,000 men of the Pennsylvania Line marched off toward the capital.

Wayne decided to follow, accompanied by Cols. Walter Stewart and Richard Butler. The next morning he dispatched to the mutineers a message, urging them to appoint one man from each regiment to negotiate with him, on his word of honor that he would do everything in his power to obtain amnesty and redress of their grievances. Late on January 3, the mutineers arrived at Princeton, where they agreed that Wayne and the colonels might lodge at a tavern near Nassau Hall—under guard—and where a 12-member Board of Sergeants the next day opened the negotiations Wayne desired. We know little about who had organized the mutiny in the first place and little about the composition and workings of the Board of Sergeants. Only three names are available: William Bowzar, secretary of the board; Daniel Connell, who was to sign the board's final communication; and one Williams, probably John Williams, who was president of the board.

Washington, who was at New Windsor, N.Y., near West Point, first heard of the mutiny through a dispatch from Wayne that reached him about noon on January 3. Concern lest the mutiny should spread or the British should respond with an attack militated against the commander in chief's inclination to travel to join Wayne in facing the mutineers. Furthermore, though Washington naturally feared concessions that might demoralize or disintegrate the rest of the army, the more he learned of Wayne's conduct, the more he concluded that on the whole Wayne was doing just what he wanted him to do. The Pennsylvania general's patience and discretion in this instance refuted his nickname, "Mad Anthony."

A committee of Congress and two delegates from the Supreme Executive Council of Pennsylvania traveled from Philadelphia to Trenton on January 5-6 to arrange to meet with the mutineers. One of the Pennsylvania delegates, Joseph Reed, president of the Supreme Executive Council, promptly made himself the central figure in the negotiations. Not only was Reed a strong personality, but the mutineers had been right to point out that their grievances could be settled only by the civil authorities. Nevertheless, when Reed, after patient and skillful bargaining, at last reached an agreement with the Board of Sergeants on January 10, it rested on terms already worked out by Wayne. Wayne's promise of amnesty was upheld. Men who had enlisted for three years or for the war were to be discharged if they had served three years and had not re-enlisted. A commission would settle disputed terms of enlistment, and if a soldier's papers were not available to verify the terms, his oath on the matter was to be accepted. Such issues as back pay, adjustment of pay for currency depreciation, and clothing shortages were to be resolved as soon as possible.

The suspense of the mutiny had been heightened by the anticipated enemy effort to capitalize upon it. On the night of January 6-7, two emissaries from General Clinton had reached the mutineers with promises of pardon, payment of the money owed them by Congress, and the privilege of refusing military service if they came over to the British. At first, the Board of Sergeants turned the emissaries over to Wayne, as evidence of the mutineers' loyalty to the Revolutionary cause.

But apparently they decided they were in no position to burn bridges and asked that the emissaries be returned to their custody. Reed arranged a compromise whereby the Board of Sergeants would hold the prisoners subject to his right to recall them. Nevertheless, there was some final haggling on January 10 when Reed demanded the emissaries as evidence that the agreement he had negotiated was accepted. The prisoners were eventually turned over, tried and convicted as spies on the 10th, and hanged on the 11th.

The same kind of ambiguity that blurred the mutineers' attitude toward Clinton's emissaries marked the whole affair, and this aspect of it returns us to its significance for the outcome of the Morristown encampments and the Revolution. When Washington learned the terms of settlement, he concluded sadly that Reed and Wayne had reached the best bargain they could, but that the result could be the dissolution of the Pennsylvania Line. The Pennsylvania enlistment records were so scattered and fragmentary that relying on the soldier's own oath where no papers were available would simply put the Pennsylvania regiments at the mercy of their members' honesty. As Washington expected, the Pennsylvania Line never recovered its old strength. The 11 Pennsylvania infantry regiments—one of which was at West Point—had been scheduled to be consolidated into six on January 1 anyway, because all had been understrength; now the six regiments failed to attain existence except on paper. But Washington's worst expectations were not realized. The men did better than feared. The Pennsylvania Line did not die. Some 1,250 infantrymen and 67 artillerymen were discharged; but almost 1,150 remained in service.

Furthermore, a high proportion of the discharged men, though exactly how many we cannot say, eventually re-enlisted. The Pennsylvania infantry formed three provisional battalions.

Still, the mutiny was bad enough. Even after it was over, and several of the benefits given the Pennsylvania troops were extended to the New Jersey Line, some of the Jerseymen mutinied at Pompton on January 20. The able Elias Dayton kept the mutiny from spreading to the rest of the New Jersey troops, and this time Washington decided he must use force to discourage further outbreaks. On January 27, loyal New England troops under the command of Maj. Gen. Robert Howe surrounded the camp of the New Jersey mutineers, compelled them to assemble without arms, and tried and sentenced three of the ringleaders to death on the spot. Two of them were executed; the third was pardoned.

Soldier's wallet with a representative sampling of authentic coins and New Jersey State bills from the Revolutionary period. The bills shown are one-, twelve-, and six-shilling notes.

Mutiny at Morristown

Washington learned early in his military career that discipline is vital to any army and that this, rather than numbers, often makes one army better than another. The difficult task of controlling his soldiers' behavior was one of the biggest problems he faced at Morristown during the winter of 1779-80.

The dreadful conditions in that winter's encampment dangerously lowered the soldiers' morale. Courts-martial found officers guilty of unbecoming conduct, theft, fraud, trading with the enemy, and unapproved absences from camp. Enlisted men were guilty of plundering, neglect of weapons, drinking, riotous conduct, desertion, and mutiny.

Of these offenses, none produced the same fear in Washington as mutiny, which could do what the British army had failed to do: destroy the Continental Army and with it the dream of American independence. The danger became all too real in May 1780, when the 1st Connecticut Brigade rose in rebellion. That uprising was quickly subdued, but Washington knew that others would follow if Congress did not provide food, clothing, and money. He was right.

During the winter of 1780-81, while most of the Continental Army was quartered at New Windsor on the Hudson River north of West Point, the veteran Pennsylvania Line, commanded by Maj. Gen. Anthony Wayne (far left), returned to Jockey Hollow. Like the rest of Washington's soldiers, the Pennsylvanians had accumulated many grievances. Wayne knew that trouble was coming and had urged the Pennsylvania authorities to remedy the problems.

On New Year's Day, 1781, tired of pleading, the Pennsylvanians mutinied. After killing one officer and wounding two others, they marched off to take their case directly to Congress. Washington wanted to deal sternly with the mutineers, but Wayne and Joseph Reed (near left), president of the Supreme Executive Council of Pennsylvania, persuaded him to let them work out an agreement that settled the dispute amicably before the mutineers reached Philadelphia.

The Revolutionary army and cause clung falteringly to life. It is little wonder that at the close of the second Morristown winter, in the spring of 1780, Knyphausen and Clinton thought they could strike into New Jersey without danger of appreciable resistance. If they had been slightly less faint-hearted themselves, and had not permitted so much vandalism by their troops, they might have been proven right: a strong thrust through Springfield might have dispersed the Continental Army. No wonder that even after his misadventure at Springfield, Clinton continued to believe the Revolution would die, if only he could prevent the French from executing some decisive stroke in the rebels' favor. The events in the Pennsylvania camps at Morristown on New Year's Day 1781 seemed to confirm this belief. After Springfield and the removal of the main army from Morristown, Washington himself wrote on July 6, 1780:
"We are, during the winter, dreaming of Independence and Peace, without using the means to become so. In the Spring, when our Recruits should be with the Army and in training, we have just discovered the necessity of calling for them. and by Fall, after a distressed, and inglorious campaign for want of them, we begin to get a few men which come in just time enough to eat our Provisions, and consume our Stores without rendering any service; that is, one year Rolls over another; and with out some change, we are hastening to our Ruin.

Between the Valley Forge winter of 1777-78 and the Morristown winter of 1779-80, the Continental Army had improved—in military professionalism and administration, in camp security, sanitation, logistics, in all the details of army life—but not enough. The im-

provement had sufficed to carry the army through a winter of far more cruelly bitter cold and winds and deeper snow than at Valley Forge, but not enough to give the Revolution an army comparable to the British in effectiveness of organization and supply, let alone in campaign and battle. Nor had the infant United States yet developed a taxation and financial system adequate to sustain an army. The Continental Army could not yet confront the British army in combat on equal terms, and the Revolution therefore remained a war of posts and encampments, not of battles. Because the army could fight only on a small scale and because it could barely sustain its life, the Revolutionary cause itself faltered—not so much because American convictions about issues and principles changed but because the parlous state of the army drained confidence that the convictions could ever be realized. For want of a nail, a horse was lost—and eventually a kingdom. For want of nails and enough other small, tangible supplies, the Revolution might have died in Morristown in 1780 and 1781.

So Clinton hoped, and so Washington feared. Both commanders believed that if the American Revolution was to achieve American independence, it was up to the French. Through 1780 and most of 1781, Washington's hopes on that score were all disappointed. The promised French army arrived but camped idly at Newport. The French fleets that visited North American waters, though less idle, seemed no match for the Royal Navy even when the French had greater numbers of ships. In the end, it was virtually a historical accident that at last fulfilled Washington's hope for the French: a series of highly fortunate and often extraordinary events, such as the only French fleet victory over the British navy in a century, all fell into place in just the right order to produce the decisive Franco-American victory at Yorktown on October 19, 1781.

Had it not been for Yorktown, the patriots might well have given up hope of ever winning the prolonged struggle and arranged a peace restoring the British Empire in America. Even if Clinton had remained cautiously inactive in New York, the Revolution might well have faded away. Despite the Continental Army's survival through the bitter winter of 1779-80, the history of the Morristown encampments of the Revolution is predominantly a gloomy tale, in keeping with the gloomy mood in which Washington led his main army away from the place.

Yet the history of the Morristown encampments remains also ambiguous. If the army had not survived at Morristown, French aid could not have helped and there would have been no Yorktown. However falteringly, the army did survive.

On February 7, 1781, after the New Jerseyans' mutiny had been subdued, Washington ordered the New Jersey Line to occupy the Morristown post on the west flank of his defensive positions around New York. In Morristown, huts were open because the remaining Pennsylvania troops had been furloughed as another part of their settlement. After Cornwallis' surrender at Yorktown, Clinton's British army stayed in New York City until a final peace was arranged, and thus New York still had to be watched. So the New Jersey Line returned to the familiar area around Morristown yet again on December 7, 1781. Elias Dayton was a brigadier now, justly enough, and in command of the little two-regiment

New Jersey Brigade. Where his men camped is uncertain. According to local tradition, it was in Jockey Hollow a short distance southeast of the Wick House. With the war languishing, Dayton's men remained almost through the next summer, until August 29, 1782. Then Washington ordered them closer to New York. The last of their sick and supplies moved within the next two weeks, and Morristown's history as a military encampment ended.

Officer's original leather covered trunk, lined with blue paper and decorated with brass tacks. The uniform and blanket are reproductions; the sword and bottle are Revolutionary era items.

Part 3

A Guide to Morristown

Visiting the Park

From George Washington's headquarters in the Ford Mansion to the rough-hewn soldier huts of Jockey Hollow, Morristown National Historical Park provides a portrait of military and civilian life in 18th-century America, illuminating the trials and triumphs of this Nation's struggle for independence during the Continental Army's winter encampments of 1777 and 1779-80.

Tours of the park can begin at either the headquarters museum or the visitor center in Jockey Hollow. At each site films about the 1779-80 encampment highlight the difficult—and often desperate—circumstances faced by Washington and his men and the effects of the army's presence on the people of this rural community.

The Ford Mansion, which contains a number of period and original furnishings, appears today much as it did when George Washington occupied it. The headquarters museum across the lawn has a rich collection of artifacts and contains a major research library on the Revolutionary era. A visit to the mansion and museum should take about one and one-half hours.

West of the mansion, Fort Nonsense rises 230 feet above the Morristown Green. From these heights, New Jersey militia scanned the eastern horizon beyond the Watchung Mountains for beacon fires that would signal British troop movements out of New York City.

Jockey Hollow, 4 miles southwest of Morristown, contains reconstructed soldier huts of the Pennsylvania Line; the Wick Farm, headquarters of Maj. Gen. Arthur St. Clair; the Grand Parade, historical site of military drills and reviews; numerous walking trails; and a visitor center. A visit to Jockey Hollow should take from one to two hours.

Military re-enactments, concerts of period music, and special activities are held in the park throughout the year. Many military programs take place near the site of the First Pennsylvania Brigade camp and the reconstructed soldier huts shown on pages 84-85. Information on park programs is available at the headquarters museum and at the visitor center in Jockey Hollow, or by writing to the Superintendent, Morristown National Historical Park, Morristown, NJ 07960.

The loop back Windsor side chair in front of the desk is among original furnishings used by General Washington in his private office at the first-floor rear of the Ford Mansion.

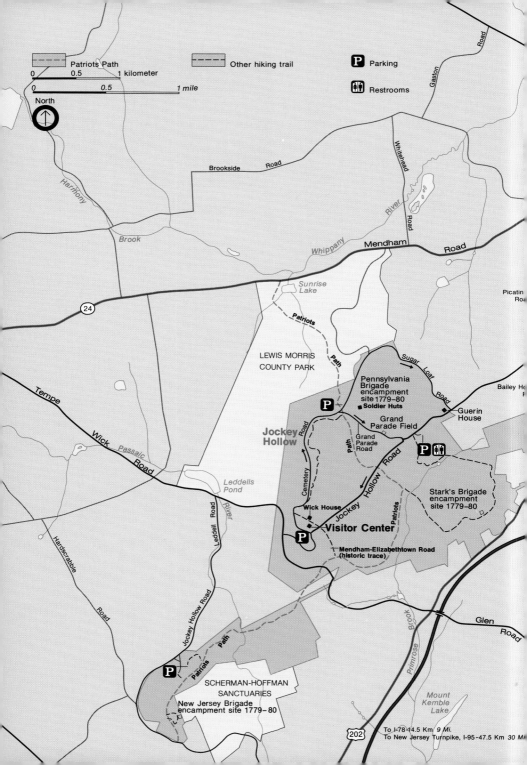

Patriots Path
Other hiking trail

P Parking

Restrooms

0   0.5   1 kilometer

0   0.5   1 mile

North

Gaston Road

Brookside   Road

Whitehead River Road

Harmony

Brook

Whippany   Mendham   Road

24

Sunrise Lake

Picatin Ro

LEWIS MORRIS
COUNTY PARK

Patriots

Path

Sugar Loaf Road

Bailey Ro

Pennsylvania
Brigade
encampment
site 1779–80
Soldier Huts

Guerin
House

Grand
Parade Field

Jockey
Hollow

Grand
Parade Road

P

Tempe

Wick

Passaic

Road

Cemetery Path

Path

Jockey Hollow Road

Stark's Brigade
encampment
site 1779–80

P

Leddells
Pond

River

Wick House

Patriots

Visitor Center

P

Leddell Road

Hardscrabble

Road

Mendham-Elizabethtown Road
(historic trace)

Brook

Glen   Road

Jockey Hollow Road

Primrose

Patriots   Path

P

SCHERMAN-HOFFMAN
SANCTUARIES

New Jersey Brigade
encampment site 1779–80

Mount
Kemble
Lake

202   To I-78–14.5 Km 9 Mi.
To New Jersey Turnpike, I-95–47.5 Km 30 Mi

Washington's Headquarters

"I certify that the Commander in Chief took up his quarters at Mrs. Ford's in Morris Town the first day of December 1779, that he left the 23rd of June 1780, and that he occupied two Rooms below, all the upper floor, Kitchen, Cellar and Stable. The Stable was built and the two rooms above Stairs finished at the public expense, and a well, which was intirely useless and filled up before, put in thorough repair by walling etc."

— Certificate of Occupation, sent to Theodosia Ford by Richard Kidder Meade, July 26, 1780.

In 1777, when the Continental Army first came to Morristown, one of the finest private dwellings in the village belonged to Col. Jacob Ford, Jr., the prosperous owner of a mine, forge, and powder mill, and an officer in the New Jersey militia. Begun in 1772 the Ford Mansion followed the Early Georgian style of architecture introduced in the colonies in 1705 with the construction of the Governor's Place in Williamsburg. This design, which became a model for 18th-century mansions in America, featured a symmetrical facade and interior room arrangement.

The mansion's main entrance is flanked by engaged ionic columns and ornate cornices and crowned with a distinguished fanlight of interlacing pattern. Inside, a spacious central hallway runs the depth of the house on both the first and second floors, and both hallways are flanked by two rooms each on the east and west sides. Kitchen, pantry, and servants' quarters occupy a two-story wing abutting the east end of the mansion.

Colonel Ford, his wife Theodosia, and their children moved into the house in 1774. Ford died here of pneumonia at the age of 39 in January 1777. At that time the mansion was serving as quarters for Delaware troops under the command of Capt. Thomas Rodney. On December 1, 1779, Theodosia Ford again opened the house to Continental troops, this time to General Washington and his military entourage for what turned out to be a seven-month stay. For 200 days the Ford Manison served as the nerve center of the Revolutionary War, where statesmen and foreign diplomats came to consult with the commander in chief.

Converting their home into a military headquarters required considerable sacrifice of privacy and comfort for Mrs. Ford and her four children, who kept only two rooms on the first floor for their own use. Timothy, age 17, Gabriel, 15, and Jacob, 8, slept in the small rear room, while 12-year-old Elizabeth shared her mother's bedchamber, which also served as the family's living and dining rooms.

To ease the burden upon the Fords, Washington ordered the construction of log buildings at each end of the mansion—the one on the east to contain a second kitchen, the one on the west to provide additional office space. Unfinished upstairs walls were plastered, and a well was repaired and walled. Huts were built nearby to shelter the 250 members of the Life Guard, who protected the headquarters.

The furnishings of the Ford Mansion today may appear restrained (if not severe) by comparison with other historic houses, but they do reflect the type of furnishings that were in the house during Washington's occupancy and provide a glimpse at the lifestyle and circumstances of a prosperous provincial family in the midst of the American Revolution.

Command Post Washington and his aides conducted the business of war in the two rooms on the west side of the first-floor hallway and also in the log structure he had built (and which no longer stands) on the west side of the mansion. The commander in chief used the front room as a conference room and staff office to meet with officers, scouts, spies, diplomats, and private citizens, and for informal discussions of military topics such as supply and recruitment problems. The room also served as an officers' mess at breakfast and dinner and, during visits by foreign envoys, as a state dining room. The rear chamber was Washington's private office, where he handled most of the correspondence that kept the Continental Army intact during the 1779-80 winter.

Upstairs, over the conference room, Martha Washington and her husband shared a handsomely furnished bedroom. Across the hallway, Washington aides Tench Tilghman, Robert Hanson Harrison, Richard Kidder Meade, James McHenry, and Alexander Hamilton occupied somewhat more spartan quarters. The Washington servants, those of the military aides, and the Ford household staff, crowded into two unheated rooms above the kitchen.

Fine examples of Chippendale furniture grace the headquarters conference room: a mahogany secretary, c. 1770, right, and a walnut veneer mirror, c. 1750, whose gilded top is shown above, right.

During their stay at the Ford mansion, Washington's aides slept on their field camp beds, which were collapsible and thus could be transported and set up with ease indoors or in the field. The camp bed frames could be curtained to provide more warmth or screening from insects. The uncurtained bed shown at left is a rare original surviving from the Revolutionary period.

The Washingtons' bedroom was Martha's daytime sitting room and parlor during the winter and spring of 1780. As in the conference room, the 18th-century American Chippendale style is well represented in the mahogany dressing table, mirror, and side chair used by Mrs. Washington. The dressing table frame is decorated with carved fretwork in Chinese motifs; flowers, leaves, and nuts ornament the table's front legs.

93

During the 1779-80 encampment, a downstairs dining room, right, became a bedroom for Theodosia Ford and her daughter Elizabeth. It also served as the family sitting and dining rooms. Mrs. Ford's three sons slept in a smaller adjoining room. The mahogany Queen Anne dropleaf table and Chippendale chairs, right foreground, were made between 1760 and 1780.

Family Quarters For Theodosia Ford and her children and servants, the once-comfortable mansion became crowded and confining with the arrival of Washington and his staff. Mrs. Ford and her family withdrew to two make-shift bedrooms, relinquishing three-quarters of their living space. There were few over-lapping activities between the headquarters staff and the Ford household; relations were formal and cordial, but boundaries were well-drawn.

One exception was the kitchen. Spacious and warm,

its large fireplace the only source of heat in the east wing, the kitchen was the shared domain of Washington and Ford servants—about 25 people in all. Scents of wood-smoke from cooking fires and candles mingled with aromas of smoked and salted meats, dried fruits and vegetables, cider, crocks of butter and other supplies stored by Mrs. Ford in an adjoining pantry to feed her household through the winter. All the daily activity and crowded conditions inevitably produced great tensions between the two kitchen staffs, and it was Washington's determination to relieve this friction that caused him to order the construction of a separate log kitchen next to this one.

The strained atmosphere of the kitchen was sympto-matic of the divided character of the Ford household during the winter of 1779-80. Another indication was the re-stricted access to the house itself. Friends calling on Mrs. Ford were required to use the outside door near the pantry; the main entrance, which was guarded by sen-tries, was reserved for official army business only.

In the Ford kitchen, above, and the separate log structure built by Washington's soldiers, breakfast, lunch, and dinner were prepared each day for nearly 30 people—still more when guests were entertained.

For the Ford children— Timothy, Gabriel, Jacob, and Elizabeth—the excitement of Washington's presence in their home compensated for many discomforts. A tutor continued their lessons, and there was time for play and games.

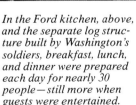

Museum and Library The museum is an important orientation point for the park and the historical events that happened here. Exhibits of numerous military and colonial artifacts, pieces of art, and audio-visual programs afford glimpses of the Continental Army in winter quarters at Morristown. The museum also houses the park library, a nationally significant repository and research facility for the Revolutionary War period. Rare and unusual books, significant diaries, military logs, and letters of soldiers, townspeople, and military and government leaders are among the more than 50,000 manuscripts and 20,000 volumes located here.

The objects shown at the right are representative of the types of items in the museum's collections: a British "Brown Bess," the most common musket of the Revolution; George Washington's agate-grip, monogrammed hunting sword; Gilbert Stuart's portrait of Washington; a three-spout brass whale-oil lamp; and a silver, pocket-size sundial compass of French origin.

Other items include Janet Clark's sampler, dated April 4, 1772, depicting the story of Adam and Eve in silk thread on linsey woolsey. The Chinese export punch bowl bears a copy of Richard Varick's membership in the Society of the Cincinnati. The carpenter's plane is from Connecticut, dated 1774. Library treasures shown above include a 1781 broadside announcing Cornwallis' surrender at Yorktown, von Steuben's drill book for the American Army, and the American Military Pocket Atlas, *published in London in 1776. At left is one of many documents signed by Washington.*

Fort Nonsense

On a clear day, from the heights of Fort Nonsense, the twin silhouettes of Manhattan's World Trade Center are visible to the east, graphically demonstrating the strategical value of this high lookout point. When the Continental Army took up residence in and around Morristown in January 1777, Washington was faced with the herculean task of gathering supplies for the coming campaign. At the same time he was confronted by the threat of a British raiding party coming out from New York to destroy those supplies. Consequently he ordered constructed, on the northern crest of Mount Kemble overlooking the Morristown Green and the Watchung Mountain ridges, a guard post accommodating 30 men.

Earthworks were afterwards added and the whole fortification served to protect American military supplies in the Morristown region throughout the remainder of the Revolution. Due to the natural barriers which made Morristown a good site for the winter camps in the first place, no British attack was ever made against the town and the "upper redoubt," as Washington called the fortification, never saw action.

The fort remained a local landmark during most of the 19th century but the purpose for which it was built became obscured. Slowly the story grew that Washington could find little useful work to keep his soldiers busy and consequently ordered them to build the fort, which, since it was supposed to have had no useful purpose, was dubbed "Fort Nonsense." Over the years this became the generally accepted story throughout the community.

That the story is more myth than reality can be readily discerned if one realizes that men and resources were limited at that time and that such idle exercises would have been, for Washington, uncharacteristically wasteful. Moreover, the name "Fort Nonsense" appears nowhere in the records until long after Washington had left Morristown. And it also seems certain that had the fort been built to keep the men busy and their morale high, some evidence of this would appear in the writings of Washington and other officers connected with the encampment. None does.

Fort Nonsense has long since crumbled and rotted away, and most of the information about its original appearance must be gathered from the accounts of 19th-century visitors to the site. One of the earliest descriptions was provided by the historian Benson J. Lossing, who stopped here in September 1848 during his long and arduous travels that produced the now-classic *Pictorial Field-Book of the American Revolution.* At that time, Lossing found prominent remains of ditches, embankments, and blockhouses, the whole "distinctly traced among the trees."

A later and more comprehensive description was given by Maj. Joseph Pierson Farley, a U.S. Army officer who in 1887, at the request of the Washington Association of New Jersey, made "a careful survey of the old Fort" and provided "a plan showing the lines... as they were originally thrown up." Farley's drawing showed an oblong fortification on a bastioned trace, with an earthen parapet and protected all around by a ditch 6 feet wide and 2 feet deep.

Today only a rough hewn block of Waterloo granite, placed there by the Washington Association in 1888, marks the site of "an earthwork built by the Continental Army."

Jockey Hollow

Seven December blizzards welcomed Washington's weary soldiers to Morristown in 1779, the onset of the worst winter of the 18th century. Nine hundred acres of timber were cleared in Jockey Hollow as the troops immediately set about building a camp of 1,200 log huts to the dimensions prescribed by Washington: 14 feet wide, 15 to 16 feet long, and about 6.5 feet high. Any non-conforming huts were to be pulled down and rebuilt to the correct specifications.

The huts, built of notched logs and chinked with clay, climbed the hillsides above the parade ground. Enlisted men's huts were arranged eight in a row, to a depth of three or four rows per regiment. Beyond were the huts of captains and subalterns, and higher still were those of field officers. These larger cabins, which were not begun until those housing the enlisted men were completed, contained two fireplaces, two chimneys, and two or more windows, and accommodated two to four officers each.

The soldiers slept 12 to a hut on built-in wooden bunks stacked three to a wall. Loose straw served as bedding, and here the men stored personal belongings such as letters from home, Bibles, and playing cards, along with clothing and other military equipage (very much like those items shown in the photograph at right). Each man carried his own eating utensils and, except for fresh bread furnished by the camp bakery, prepared his own meals from the scanty rations provided. Soldier diaries of the encampment make frequent, rueful, and bitter note of the many days when no rations were available. These shortages were not suffered by the civilian population, but were the product of a young and weak Congress' failure to both appreciate the severity of conditions at Morristown and to set up an adequate system of procurement and supply. Rampant inflation, a virtually worthless Continental currency, and the weather bedevilled the best efforts of Washington and his staff to feed and clothe the army.

Revolving enlistments created further headaches. Many of the troops Washington struggled to maintain through the winter became eligible for discharge in the spring. Thus on the eve of re-engaging the enemy, a helpless and frustrated Washington could do nothing but stand and watch those with a semblance of training vanish—and raw recruits replace them.

Hungry, desperate soldiers habitually plundered local farmers and merchants, who often charged exorbitant prices for the food they sold the army. Drunkenness was common. For many of the troops in Jockey Hollow the tug of hearth and home and fields to be tended was too strong to resist. They just walked away from the cold, the hunger, and the war—1,066 soldiers deserted during the 1779-80 encampment. Other serious offenses included assault, trading with the enemy, gambling, and the attempted mutiny by two Connecticut regiments in May 1780.

Washington judiciously refrained from exacting the full measure of military punishment for every breach of discipline, mindful of the dreadful privations endured by both enlisted men and officers. Alert to possibilities for recreation that could give some relief from the cold, hunger, and monotony of camp routine, he encouraged masonic activities and declared holidays, such as celebrating St. Patrick's Day, the latter thanks to Irish recognition of American independence.

The Wick House A short walk from the Jockey Hollow Visitor Center is the house occupied during the Revolution by apple farmer Henry Wick and his family. It was also the headquarters of Maj. Gen. Arthur St. Clair, commander of the Pennsylvania Line, during the winter of 1779-80.

The Wicks had moved from Long Island to Morris County in 1748. The house, built about 1750, is a Cape-Cod style, more typical of New England than of New Jersey. It features a large central chimney serving three fireplaces, a wood construction, and a spacious kitchen. The interior walls are wood-sheathed, the front wall is shingled, and the side and rear walls are weatherboarded. All in all, the house reflects the informality of an 18th-century rural household in contrast to the more imposing grandeur of gentry residences like the Ford Mansion.

Mary Cooper Wick, age 61, and her 21-year-old daughter Temperance were the only family members living on the 1,400-acre farm during the second Continental Army encampment. (Henry Wick, 72, was serving as a volunteer with the Morris County cavalry.) The Wick parlor became General St. Clair's office, while a small adjoining bedchamber, sometimes used as a spinning room, served for his sleeping quarters. His aides probably slept in the dining room or parlor.

Furnishings appropriate to the second and third quarters of the 18th century, and to the locale have been placed in the house. And a few outbuildings have been reconstructed on their original sites.

Garden and Orchard A kitchen garden next to the house provided herbs and plants for medicines, dyes, seasonings, polishes, and cleansers. It also supplied fruits and vegetables for the Wick's table. The orchards yielded a bounty of apples for cider-making, cooking, and eating. The present garden is a recreation of an 18th-century kitchen garden, based on research by New Jersey members of the Herb Society of America.

Kitchen garden herbs include Lady's Bed Straw, top, used for mattress stuffing and dye; chives, center, a wild onion substitute; and Lamb's Ear, bottom, whose leaves were placed on cuts to speed healing.

St. Clair's Quarters The presence of General St. Clair in the Wick house, like that of Washington in the Ford Mansion, imposed unaccustomed hardships on the rural household of his hosts. Mary Wick and her daughter Temperance kept to two rooms for the six months St. Clair lived there. A Scotsman educated at Edinburgh University, St. Clair later served in the Continental Congress from 1785-87 and as governor of the Northwest Territory from 1789-1802.

During his stay here, General St. Clair converted the Wick's parlor to use as an office and meeting room. He probably ate most of his meals here and toiled over many of the problems common to a brigade commander in winter, such as enlistments, the snow and cold, and provisions. A small room off to the left was used as his sleeping room.

Pennsylvania Line The Pennsylvania Line consisted of the First and Second Pennsylvania Brigades commanded by Maj. Gen. Arthur St. Clair. These troops served from the 1775 invasion of Canada to the final victory over the British at Yorktown in 1781.

At Morristown in 1779-80, the First Pennsylvania Brigade, under Brig. Gen. William Irvine, numbered 1,290 men of the 1st, 2d, 7th, and 10th Pennsylvania Regiments. Their huts were located west of the junction of Jockey Hollow and Sugar Loaf Roads on the western slope of Sugar Loaf Hill. Reconstructions of several huts, one of which is shown at bottom right, mark the site of the brigade's encampment and that of the Second Pennsylvania Brigade commanded by Col. Francis Johnston in the absence of Brig. Gen. Anthony Wayne. Numbering 1,112 men, this latter brigade was comprised of the 3rd, 5th, 6th, and 9th regiments.

The two main tasks of the soldiers who camped here during the 1779-80 Morristown encampment, like those regiments and brigades who camped elsewhere, were drill and training, and guard duty—the first to maintain the physical condition and combat readiness of the troops and the second to warn of any British activity. Daily troop inspections, which included matters of personal grooming and cleanliness, emphasized the proper care and maintenance of weapons and cartridge boxes.

Grand Parade The Grand Parade, shown here, was an important part of encampment life, and a center of military activities. A field between the Pennsylvania and New York campsites was cleared to provide an area for military inspections, drill, reviews, ceremonial functions, executions, and the lesser punishments of running the gauntlet and whippings.

New Jersey Brigade The New Jersey Brigade, led by Brig. Gen. William Maxwell, arrived at Eyre's Forge on December 17, 1779, and began to build huts along Indian Graves Brook, shown at right. Composed of the 1st, 2d, 3rd, and Spencer's Regiments, the brigade's 1,314 soldiers guarded the southern route into the main garrison from their position on the north side of Hardscrabble Road between Basking Ridge and Mendham.

Stark's Brigade Camped on the east slope of Mount Kemble were the 1,270 officers and men of Brig. Gen. John Stark's brigade, which included units from three New England states. Its components were the 2d Rhode Island Regiment, two Connecticut regiments under Cols. Henry Sherburne and Samuel Webb, and a Massachusetts regiment under Col. Henry Jackson. A fifth regiment, Livingston's Canadians, was on detached service. The monument marks the brigade's encampment site.

The First National Historical Park

Unwilling to see one of the memorable places of the Revolution fade into oblivion, four Jerseymen snatched the Ford Mansion from an uncertain fate one summer day in 1873. They bid $25,000 at auction and saved the old landmark from going the way of a boarding house or worse. They expected to hold the property in trust until the State could acquire it as a historical site But there was, alas, little sentiment in the legislature to take over the house and operate it as a museum.

Perhaps it was just as well. Left to their own resources, the founders organized a group of likeminded Morris County men into the Washington Association. Their purpose was avowedly patriotic: to make the mansion into a place in which visitors could contemplate the past and in times of danger find inspiration. To be sure, the association did eventually receive some public help. The State granted a liberal charter that conferred tax-free status on the house and a small annual stipend in return for keeping the house open to the public "at all proper times."

The Washington Association was far more than a caretaker. It set about collecting historical "relics," encouraged scholarship, and over the next half century assembled an important collection of books and manuscripts. One delightful custom established in the first years was the annual meeting on Washington's Birthday. From 1887 on, the meetings centered not on long speeches by dignitaries but on talks related to Washington and the Revolution. Among the distinguished scholars who have addressed the membership are Woodrow Wilson (1903), Henry Cabot Lodge (1916), Carl Van Doren (1944), and Douglas Southall Freeman (1951).

The house has never lacked for visitors. In the 1890s visits ran about 9,000 a year. By 1930 the figure was over 31,000. Many persons came on trains chartered for the day out of Newark or New York City. They found much to see. Rooms were stuffed with memorabilia—weapons and gear; maps, prints, and paintings; furniture from many eras; and a dazzling variety of curiosities—all carefully labeled. Locals joked that the house was "Morristown's attic."

The truth was that the association was pinched between rising expenses and the expectations of the traveling public. A depression was on, and the trustees had neither the money nor the time to do all that they wanted. In 1921, for example, they turned down the gift of the Wick house for lack of money to maintain it.

At this point, a number of ideas—personal, local, and national—converged into a movement to create a historical park under the jurisdiction of the Federal government. Three figures stand out. Mayor Clyde Potts was determined that the Jockey Hollow woodlands should be preserved intact and not built over. Lloyd W. Smith, a wealthy collector of Washingtoniana, led a committee to rescue the "sacred ground" and eventually wound up buying most of the tract himself. Horace Albright, director of the National Park Service, was quick to see the need for his agency to become more involved in historical preservation in the East. The several owners—the association, the town (which had title to Fort Nonsense), and Lloyd Smith—gladly pooled their properties and offered them to the government. With so much local support, the proposal sailed through Congress. President Herbert Hoover signed the legislation into law on March 2, 1933, establishing Morristown as the first National Historical Park.

The stereo card above shows the Ford Mansion late in the 19th century after its rescue by the Washington Association. In 1888 the Association's first annual Washington's Birthday meeting was held in the house, with 45 of its 250 members present. That year also the group placed the commemorative boulder and plaque, left, atop Mount Kemble to mark the site of Fort Nonsense and removed a balustrade piazza from the Ford Mansion, returning the building to its original simplicity.

The Wick House, which remained in family ownership until 1871, is shown at left in 1933 when the National Park Service acquired the property. After thorough architectural research, the house was restored to what was believed to be its condition during the 1779-80 Continental Army encampment. In the 1930s, under Park Service direction, Civilian Conservation Corps workers, above, carried out archeological digs in Jockey Hollow.

Sites of Related Interest

**Valley Forge
National Historical Park, Pa.**
Site of the Continental Army's 1777-78 winter encampment. Here the army lost nearly 2,500 men to starvation, disease, and the cold. Washington's headquarters building, several officers' quarters, many reconstructed soldier huts, and park programs highlight the story of the first large winter encampment of the Revolution. Located 100 miles south of Morristown, off Pa. 23.

New Windsor Cantonment, N.Y.
Site of the Continental Army's 1782-83 winter encampment. It was here that the Treaty of Paris ending the war was announced to the troops. The site contains Washington's headquarters, Gen. Henry Knox's headquarters, and a reconstructed encampment area. Located at Newburgh, N.Y., about 80 miles north of Morristown on the west bank of the Hudson River off U.S. 9W.

Ringwood Manor State Park, N.J.
The site of the 18th-century home and ironworks of Robert Erskine, mapmaker to the Continental Army and friend of Washington. Erskine drew some of the earliest maps of the Morristown area. His forge also provided cannon and shot for the Revolution. The State park contains Ringwood Manor, with its extensive landscaping and formal gardens, and many artifacts. It is also a wildlife sanctuary. Located north of Pompton Lakes at Ringwood, N.J., on N.J. 511 near the New Jersey-New York border.

Trenton, N.J.
Site of Washington's surprise attack on Col. Johann Rall's Hessian garrison on Christmas night, 1776. The spot where the American artillery began the battle is marked by the Trenton Battle Monument at the junction of N. Broad and Warren Streets, and Brunswick, Pennington, and Princeton Avenues. The Old Barracks, occupied by Rall's troops at the time of the attack, still stands near the State Capitol on South Willow Street opposite West Front. Trenton is about 60 miles south of Morristown via U.S. 206 or U.S. 1.

Princeton Battlefield Park, N.J.
Scene of the second phase of Washington's surprise 1776-77 winter offensive against the British. Princeton Battlefield Park preserves part of the land on which the battle was fought. Nassau Hall, the city's most important landmark, is now part of Princeton University. It was here in 1781 that mutinous Pennsylvania soldiers from the Jockey Hollow encampment negotiated their grievances. Nassau Hall also served as the national capital for a while in 1783 when Congress occupied it after fleeing Philadelphia to escape the threat of embittered war veterans. Princeton is about 40 miles south of Morristown via U.S. 206.

Springfield, N.J.
Site of the June 23, 1780, battle in which new Jersey militia and Continental troops stopped British troops intent on destroying American military supplies at Morristown. Historical markers, old houses, and churches are among the important landmarks of the battle. Located about 15 miles southeast of Morristown on N.J. 24.

For Further Reading

Bill, Alfred Hoyt. *New Jersey and the Revolutionary War.* Princeton: D. Van Nostrand, 1964.

Boatner, Mark M., III. *Encyclopedia of the American Revolution.* New York: David McKay, 1966.

Boatner, Mark M., III. *Landmarks of the American Revolution.* Harrisburg: Stackpole Books, 1973.

Fleming, Thomas J. *The Forgotten Victory: The Battle for New Jersey—1780.* New York: Reader's Digest Press, 1973.

Flexner, James T. *Washington: The Indispensable Man.* Boston: Little, Brown, 1974.

Lundin, Leonard. *Cockpit of the Revolution: The War for Independence in New Jersey.* Princeton: Princeton University Press, 1940.

Peterson, Harold L. *The Book of the Continental Soldier.* Harrisburg: Stackpole Books, 1968.

Scheer, George F., and Hugh F. Rankin, eds. *Rebels and Redcoats.* Cleveland and New York: World Publishing Company, 1957.

Shelley, Fred, ed. "Ebenezer Hazard's Diary: New Jersey during the Revolution." *New Jersey History,* XC (Autumn 1978), 169-80.

Sherman, Andrew M. *Historic Morristown, New Jersey: The Story of Its First Century.* Morristown: Howard Publishing Company, 1905.

Smith, Samuel Stelle. *Winter at Morristown 1779-1780: The Darkest Hour.* Monmouth Beach, N.J.: Philip Freneau Press, 1979.

Thacher, James. *A Military Journal during the American Revolutionary War, from 1775 to 1783.* New York: Arno Press, 1969.

Ward, Christopher. *The War of the Revolution.* Ed. John R. Alden. 2 vols. New York: Macmillan, 1952.

Wright, Robert K., Jr. *The Continental Army.* Washington: Center of Military History, United States Army, 1983.

Handbook 120

The National Park Service expresses it appreciation
to all those persons who made the preparation
and production of this handbook possible.

Texts
Russell F. Weigley, who wrote the text in Part 2 of
this booklet, teaches history at Temple University,
Philadelphia, Pa. Among his numerous works are
*Towards An American Army: Military Thought
from Washington to Marshall, History of the United
States Army,* and *The American Way of War.*
   George F. Scheer, who wrote about "The Winter
Soldiers" in Part 1, is a long-time student of the
American Revolution. He is co-author of *Rebels and
Redcoats* and editor of *Private Yankee Doodle,* a
narrative by Joseph Plumb Martin, one of the soldiers
who endured the 1779-80 winter at Morristown.

Illustrations
Anne S.K. Brown Military Collection, Providence,
Rhode Island: 22 (Howe); Ross Chapple: 14-15; R.R.
Donnelley Cartographic Service: 20-21, 88-89; George
Fistrovich: cover, 4-5, 16, 32, 39, 43, 45, 50 (Steuben
manual), 53, 56-57, 64 (ledger), 66, 75, 79, 83, 105
(St. Clair's Office); Historical Society of Pennsylvania:
22 (King George III);Independence National Historical
Park: 30, 49 (Ternant, Duportail), 58, 64 (Greene),
80 (Wayne, Reed), 105 (St. Clair); Morristown Na-
tional Historical Park: 36 (Arnold Tavern), 87, 109;
Musees Nationaux Paris: 69; Mount Vernon Ladies
Association: 19; National Army Museum, London:
22 (Clinton); National Portrait Gallery, London: 22
(Cornwallis); George Neumann: 50 (military manuals);
New-York Historical Society: 34-35; New York State
Historical Association, Cooperstown: 48-49 (Steuben);
Samuel S. Smith, *Winter at Morristown: The Darkest
Hour:* 37 (sketch of Ford Mansion by Phyllis Mitchell);
Staples & Charles: 84-85, 86, 91, 92-93, 94-95, 96-97,
98, 101, 102-3, 104, 106-7; Don Troiani: 7, 10-11, 26-27,
36-37 (Life Guards), 40-41, 50-51, 59, 65, 72-73, 80-81.

National Park Service
U.S. Department of the Interior

As the Nation's principal conservation agency, the Department of the Interior has responsibility for most of our nationally owned public lands and natural resources. This includes fostering the wisest use of our land and water resources, protecting our fish and wildlife, preserving the environmental and cultural values of our national parks and historical places, and providing for the enjoyment of life through outdoor recreation. The Department assesses our energy and mineral resources and works to assure that their development is in the best interest of all our people. The Department also has a major responsibility for American Indian reservation communities and for people who live in island territories under U.S. administration.

Morristown

Official National Park Handbook